SECRET LEICESTER

STEPHEN BUTT

AMBERLEY

First published 2013

Amberley Publishing
The Hill, Stroud
Gloucestershire, GL5 4EP

www.amberley-books.com

Copyright © Stephen Butt, 2013

The right of Stephen Butt to be identified as the
Author of this work has been asserted in accordance
with the Copyrights, Designs and Patents Act 1988.

ISBN 978 1 4456 0760 3

British Library Cataloguing in Publication Data.
A catalogue record for this book is available from
the British Library.

Typeset in 9.5pt on 12pt Celeste.
Typesetting by Amberley Publishing.
Printed in the UK.

CONTENTS

Richard III Statue
The bronze statue of Richard III by James Walter Butler RA was erected in Castle Gardens near St Nicholas Circle, close to the site of the bridge across which his corpse was carried after the Battle of Bosworth Field on 22 August 1485. It was commissioned and paid for by members of the Richard III Society, and was unveiled on 31 July 1980 by Princess Alice, Duchess of Gloucester.

INTRODUCTION

The history of a city often lies hidden. We may see the major historical structures such as the Jewry Wall, the Newarke Gateway and the medieval churches, but there is much of the history of Leicester that tells the story of the people of the city across the centuries and yet remains hidden from view.

There are exceptions. Sometimes a structure is so familiar to us, perhaps because we pass it every day, that it becomes part of the contemporary landscape and its historical significance and context is overlooked. How many railway travellers who park at Leicester's London Road station see the remnants of the earlier Campbell Street station? How many motorists driving along Sparkenhoe Street and over the Swain Street bridge see the gates to the former Leicester workhouse? How many motorists parking in the car park next to New Street recognise the retaining wall that dates in part to when the church of the Greyfriars was still standing? How many students at De Montfort University working in the Hawthorn Building notice the arches of the fourteenth-century church of St Mary of the Annunciation in the Newarke?

These somewhat 'secret' artefacts and structures are the subject of this book. Behind every façade, in every street, there is a history to be discovered and a story to be told. Some of the elements of the city's past have been erased by clumsy redevelopment or neglect, but such is the history of every town. However, in Leicester it is still possible to uncover surprising visual evidence of our heritage simply by opening a door or lifting a stone, or by comparing an old photograph or drawing with the present-day scene.

The history of Leicester is a long and unbroken narrative, the first chapter of which was written into the landscape long before the arrival of the Romans. Today, that history is being rewritten line by line. The groundbreaking (in more ways than one) archaeological investigation of the Greyfriars area of Leicester in the summer of 2012 proved that an urban car park, familiar to thousands, can reveal archaeology that can rewrite the history books and challenge the legend and assumptions of the past. Consider the hundreds, perhaps thousands, of children who have stood in the playground of the former Alderman Newton's School building in St Martin's, later an annexe to Leicester Grammar School, and were so close to the remains of Richard III.

This book is intended to complement the written record and the detailed and painstaking research of archaeologists. Instead, the less familiar, the seldom seen and the almost unknown but usually very accessible will take centre stage. It includes views that are now lost, many having disappeared as recently as the first decade of the twenty-first century, and it also records the buildings and monuments that have survived but are often hidden from public view.

Cities are made by men and women, but their footsteps through time are sometimes more transient than the bricks and mortar of their age. So although the street names have survived, there is little left in the landscape of Leicester to connect us, for instance, directly with the streets and buildings that Joseph Carey Merrick knew in the latter part of the nineteenth century. Similarly, the man after whom Merrick was named, the Baptist preacher and missionary William Carey, moved to Leicester in 1789, but there is now very little evidence of his time in the city and only a badly degraded stone bust set into a wall near St Nicholas Circle to commemorate his achievements.

The pace of change of the built environment is increasing. It is probable that this volume will be out of date by the time it is published, but, to use a photographic metaphor, it may still serve as a snapshot of how Leicester in the first decade of the twenty-first century can recognise and value its long heritage.

Stephen Butt

The Greyfriars Wall

This wall behind buildings in Peacock Lane is now the boundary of a car park. Although much defaced and frequently repaired, the oldest parts of this structure date to the time when the church of the Greyfriars was standing.

Wyggeston's Hospital

The original hospital, founded in 1513, was built on land between St Martin's churchyard and Highcross Street, now the car park of St Martin's House. The south-east buttress of St Martin's can be seen on the far right of this photograph, which dates to around 1870.

The Nag's Head
This old inn was situated near the junction of Guildhall Lane and Highcross Street, now Applegate. It was demolished to make way for the construction of the Wyggeston Boys' School in 1872.

Roger Wigston's House
Standing opposite the Nag's Head, this house was built by a member of the Wyggeston family. It has survived partly due to being obscured, and therefore protected, by the late Georgian residence built in front of it.

one

CONNECTING WITH THE PAST

There are many channels through which we can connect with the past. The basis of our interpretation of past events must be the physical evidence and the documentary record, but both may not always be present, and neither can necessarily tell the full story.

Scientific analysis is objective; it relies on precise, measured data that can be checked and retested for accuracy. By comparison, written material usually provides a broader context to the cold facts, and some written evidence, as in diaries and recorded oral history, can offer a more personal history and a journey of emotional experience.

Science can now tell us with a degree of certainty the precise disease that caused the physical abnormalities of Joseph Carey Merrick, the so-called 'Elephant Man' of Leicester, but to gain an understanding of how he perceived his life and those around him we need to turn to his own writings. Even today we can see the gateposts of the Leicester workhouse through which Merrick limped, not once but twice in his teenage years, and we can consult the official records of the institution as well as the census returns. But to gain a measure of his self-belief and his relationship with those who were able to help him is still a challenge.

The sophisticated, painstaking and highly detailed research by the University of Leicester that led to the identification of the remains of Richard III in the former church of the Greyfriars in Leicester in February 2013 demonstrated that the professional application of scientific tests can provide an incredible amount of information about the events of the past. The team's analysis was able to explain in detail how the monarch died and which of the many wounds was the mortal blow. Much more information has been deduced from the research that will take years to formulate into a final published report but will address such questions as whether the King was facing his attacker at the moment of his death, and what might have happened to his body as it was removed from the field of battle and taken back to Leicester.

The King's skull was studied and photographed with the latest three-dimensional scanning technology and a variety of other techniques, but no amount of scientific research can presume to enter into the mind of the man. True, it is possible to deduce from the evidence that, for instance, he was courageous on the battlefield, but archaeology and science cannot relate to us his thoughts and attitudes. The fine archaeology has located the 'lost' church of Greyfriars, but it is more difficult to find out how the friars felt in August 1485 when they were presented with a corpse that three or four days previously had been the King of England.

Turning to the documentary record, we know that there were several burials before that of Richard III in the area of the choir of the church of Greyfriars. These included Gilbert Luenor, the founder of the friary, and his wife Ellen. There were others, including, probably, Sir William Moton of Peckleton and at least three senior and respected friars of the past. All these individuals were laid to rest sometime between 1230 and 1330, but then, after a space of more than a century, Richard was interred beside them.

On his return to Leicester, lying naked and thrown face down over a horse, Richard's body was carried to the church of the Annunciation of St Mary in the Newarke, a Lancastrian stronghold adjacent to Leicester Castle. Here, a century earlier, John of Gaunt had ruled, from whom both Richard and Henry Tudor descended.

At the church, Richard's body was laid out 'in state', most certainly as a message to the town and the country that he was indeed dead. Some three days later, the body was handed over to the friars. It was a short journey, a matter of yards, from the Newarke to the precinct of the friars – out through the Newarke Gateway and left into the town through the south gate. Almost immediately, the procession, or perhaps the horse and cart, would have been on Franciscan land.

At the beginning of the century the Franciscans in Leicester had suffered a frightening blow. In 1402, the Franciscans' support for Richard II had led to dire consequences. One of their ranks confessed to Henry IV that eleven friars of Leicester, including the Master of Divinity and Warden of the House, Richard Friseley, had conspired in favour of the deposed Richard II. The consequence was devastating for Leicester. Eight friars and the Master of Divinity were arrested and taken to London for trial. They were all executed.

Consider the effect on this small community of quiet men. The death of their elders would have caused sadness and ceremony but also some fear for the future and unease with regard to succession. The Franciscan friars of Leicester had to face the future without their respected

The James Went Building

Known as the 'barcode building' because of its unusual window design, the James Went building was constructed on an area of Magazine Square in the Newarke. It was demolished in 2004. The floors were connected by a paternoster lift.

The Leicester Pageant, 1932

A candid image of the famous Leicester Pageant of 1932, by the Leicester artist and photographer George Moore Henton; it is typical of his style. The location is outside the Hawthorn Building in the Newarke. The Leicester School of Art designed and made most of the hundreds of costumes.

leadership. One result of these events was that a general chapter of the Franciscans, held at Leicester, issued a decree that forbade any of the Franciscan Order from speaking out against the king.

Did this decree mean *the* king of England at that time or *any* king of England? When the victorious Henry Tudor came into Leicester after the battle at Bosworth Field in 1485, did the friars remember that decree? The newly proclaimed Henry VII was ordering that Richard should be buried within the walls of the friary, alongside the men and women who had played an important spiritual role in its creation. Did the political and spiritual stance of the friars mean that they actively sought to care for and protect Richard's body? Or did they bow to the rule of the new king, remembering the devastating events that followed the last occasion on which they had challenged a new monarch?

The archaeological investigation of Greyfriars has greatly increased our knowledge of this area of the city. It is now possible to stand in the graveyard of the Cathedral of St Martin's, look towards the south and visualise the friary church nearby. The old wall behind the façades of St Martin's and Peacock Lane, defining another surface car park, may now be seen in a different light, possibly as part of the structure of the church.

The presence of the Franciscans in Leicester connects the town with Italy in the twelfth century and the very origins of the Franciscan tradition. St Francis of Assisi died in 1226. Two years earlier, the first of his missionary friars had reached England. Agnellus of Pisa, founder of the English Franciscan Province, landed in Dover on 10 September 1230. It is known that the friary in Leicester was in existence by 1230, though possibly not in the same building as the one discovered by the excavations in August 2012. It is therefore very possible that the older men of the friary in Leicester had actually met St Francis. It was his teaching that became their teaching and led to their later brethren challenging Henry IV. There is no doubt that the same theology and principles were still valid and respected in 1485 when another King Henry presented them with another deposed King Richard.

There is a further coincidence of dates that connects another major figure in Leicester's history to that defining moment on the evening of 22 August 1485. As a young man of just eighteen years, William Wyggeston the younger would almost certainly have witnessed the return to Leicester of the remnants of Richard's army as well as the Tudor escort that brought Richard's body back over the river and into the town. William was the son of a mayor and leading burgess of Leicester and would have understood the significance of the events being played out before his eyes. He had been born on the very edge

The Town Hall and Town Hall Square
Leicester's modest and pleasing town hall was designed by local architect Francis Hames and completed in 1876. This lantern slide dates to about 1896. The fountain, donated by former mayor Israel Hart and also designed by Hames, was unveiled in 1879.

Market Street and Welford Place
This view, from the 1870s, is of Joseph Johnson's department store, now Fenwicks, which was built in 1880 by Isaac Barradale. It is seen from the corner of Wellington Street and Welford Place, looking towards Market Street and Belvoir Street.

of Franciscan land in Leicester, and his great foundation, Wyggeston's Hospital, was later to be built on land previously in the ownership of Greyfriars. It lay so close to the place where Richard was to be buried that its tower no doubt cast a shadow over the hospital and its precincts. William Dugdale's *Monasticon Anglicanum* of 1655 relates that:

> In 1513 the King's Letters patent were obtained, by William, Thomas and Roger Wigston, for founding the Hospital of St Ursula, now called Wigston's Hospital, on ground which was in the precincts of the Grey Friars; to which, in 1520, William Fisher, the first master of that Hospital, obtained the addition of St Francis Garden.

The garden was on land to the west of the hospital, facing Highcross Street, and Greyfriars donated the land free of charge. Less than twenty years later, the Franciscans were to forfeit their land and holdings to the Crown. The garden was not always to be a place of tranquillity. Later, buildings were constructed along Highcross Street, including the famous Nag's Head Inn which survived until 1872 when the Wyggeston foundation elected to demolish the hospital and construct a school on the same site.

In the mid-nineteenth century, photography began to provide a record of the past. A fine record of Leicester's buildings and events was created by George Moore Henton (1861–1924), who was both an artist and a photographer. A local man, born in Regent Road, Leicester, Henton took many thousands of artistic photographs of Leicester. His collection is now in the Record Office for Leicestershire, Leicester and Rutland, in Wigston.

Several local artists associated with the Leicester College of Art have also provided a legacy of attractive and reliable images of Leicester's past. These include the first headmaster of the school, Wilmot Pilsbury (1840–1908). His home in Stoneygate, which was designed by Leicester's great Arts and Crafts architect, Isaac Barradale, includes an artist's studio on the upper floor, lit by natural light. Pilsbury himself provided some of the stucco decoration on the front elevation of the house. Other local topographic artists whose works can be seen today include John Fulleylove (1845–1908), Thomas Elgood (1845–1912) and George Elgood (1851–1943). Together, these artists and photographers have left a true connection with the past – often shown through romantic and artistic eyes, but nevertheless a reliable record of Leicester as it was perceived by them and in their time.

two

BENEATH THE NEWARKE

An early, revolutionary view of the universe and a precious thorn, said to be from Christ's crown of thorns, make up the hidden heart of the Newarke.

It has always been a special place, and separate from the town of Leicester. The buildings that influence its character today are a mix of the modern and the medieval, and although some may not merit an architectural award, they do all speak of different and specific eras in the precinct's long history, as do the structures that lie beneath them.

Although it is thought by some that Magazine Square in the Newarke has always been an open space, the view today is probably more open and less cluttered than at any time in its long history. Arguably the last time that a substantial expanse of open land could be seen in this location was before the construction of the church of the Annunciation of St Mary in the first decades of the fourteenth century.

In recent years, the Newarke has developed into the campus of De Montfort University, a still-developing landscape that has seen new buildings rise and others, inherited from the former Leicester Polytechnic from which the university was born, refurbished. It is largely the presence of a powerful place of learning that has ensured the area still has a different ambience from the nearby central area of the city of Leicester. Until the nineteenth century it lay outside the old walled Borough of Leicester, beyond its jurisdiction and exempt from some of its taxes. Even now it has an atmosphere of secluded separateness.

The 'New Work'

The Earls of Leicester and Lancaster, who had possessed the adjacent castle and its environs since the twelfth century, probably owned the land that was to become their Newarke or 'new work'. In 1330 or 1331, Henry Grosmont, 3rd Earl of Lancaster and a grandson of Henry III and Eleanor of Provence, founded a hospital here for fifty poor or infirm persons, which he chose to locate immediately outside the town but close to his castle walls. It was well provided for and well organised.

His son Henry, the 4th Earl and later 1st Duke of Lancaster, developed his father's plans with considerable flair and enthusiasm, adding greatly to the hospital buildings to provide accommodation for a further fifty people and creating a large and richly endowed chantry college. In 1349, Henry had been arrested in Germany and held to ransom by the Duke of Brunswick. On his release, Henry accused Brunswick of improper conduct. Brunswick responded by challenging him to a duel, but pulled out of the contest at the last moment and eventually offered an apology to Lancaster through the King of France. Following this incident, it is said that many rich gifts were offered to Henry, but he would accept only one, a single thorn, said to be from the crown of thorns worn by Jesus at the crucifixion. It was later to be enshrined in the church of St Mary of the Newarke.

Henry's new college was a major establishment for its time, with 12 canons, 13 vicars, 3 clerks, 6 choristers and 10 attendants to care for 100 poor and sick people, supported by chantry priests and all presided over by a dean.

It was dedicated to St Mary and became known as St Mary's of the *New Work* to distinguish it from the older college of the nearby church of St Mary de Castro, which lay just inside the town and opposite the castle. The church was completed in 1354 and was later to be described by the antiquary, poet and traveller John Leland, who visited Leicester sometime between 1535 and 1543, as 'not very great, but ... exceeding fair'.

The east end of the church, a sacred place where those who had a special association with the college could be honoured after their death, became what has been described as 'one of the great tomb houses of England'. The 'Good Duke', Henry, Duke of Lancaster, died in 1361, probably a victim of the Black Death. He lay on the north side of the altar in the place usually set aside for founders. On the opposite side lay his father, Earl Henry of Lancaster, who had died in 1345. Two of the duke's sons lay to the west of their father.

Also buried in a place of honour were Mary de Bohun, the first wife of Henry Bolingbroke, later Henry IV, who died in 1394; Constance, the second wife of John of Gaunt and daughter of Peter, King of Castile and Leon, 'in a tomb of marble with an image of brass like a queen on it'; and, in the adjoining space, all three Wyggeston brothers – William, Roger and Thomas – who had given so much of their wealth to the town and its people.

In the seventeenth century, the Newarke became a popular residential area for Leicester's wealthier citizens. The attraction of the area was the group of substantial buildings left by the canons and clergy of the religious house into which they could move. But also, as any estate agent would now emphasise, it was a secluded area protected by boundary walls, and the cost of living there was lower than in the rest of the town because the area was not under the jurisdiction of the corporation.

The borough tried on several occasions over more than two centuries to establish its claim over the Newarke, but it remained steadfastly independent of the town until well into the nineteenth century. The turning point in the prosperity and identity of the area came in the middle of the nineteenth century, when urbanisation came to the Newarke. In 1898, a new road bridge was constructed across the River Soar, which turned the narrow meandering route of the Newarke into a busy highway and resulted in the demolition of many of the older buildings that had for so long epitomised the character of the place. The Victorian development of the Newarke resulted in factories being built alongside medieval chantry houses and a Midland Red bus station next to the fourteenth-century Newarke Gateway.

The church, its college and the community it served were to prosper for almost 200 years until the time of the Dissolution of the Monasteries, a world within a world, secluded to some degree but not cut off from the wider community in the expanding town of Leicester. Indeed, the dominating architecture of the Newarke or Magazine Gateway was intended as a statement of power and authority and never served as a fortification or a means of protecting the sanctity of the Newarke from its more worldly neighbours.

In 1538, Leicester Abbey was surrendered to the Crown, but as far as the Newarke was concerned, Henry VIII stayed his hand. The King was seemingly unwilling to destroy a religious house so closely connected with his Lancastrian ancestors. For a while, the College of the Newarke was reprieved. But its community was living on borrowed time. Perhaps inevitably, after Henry's death the college was suppressed by Edward VI under the 1547 Act for the Dissolution of Chantries. Within a comparatively short space of time almost all the buildings were destroyed, with the sole exception of the hospital and a fragment of the church, which then was to vanish from sight and living memory.

The destruction of the college and church appears to have been very thorough. However, the hospital was spared, though under a different regime. It still exists today in modern facilities in nearby Western Boulevard; the new buildings were constructed in 1995. The old hospital building was purchased by De Montfort University and now houses some of its administrative departments. It has been rebuilt on several occasions, and the chapel, where sacred music is still performed on occasions, is the only part of the original almshouse to survive. A stipend of £246 *per annum* is still paid by the Duchy of Lancaster to the hospital, maintaining an arrangement unbroken since its foundation in 1331. The Chancellor of the Duchy of Lancaster appoints the hospital's chaplain by letters patent on behalf of the Queen.

The only other survival of the college above ground is one of the original gateways into the Newarke. However, two arches of the church, with their retaining columns, survived but became buried. They were protected from later destruction because they had been incorporated into the supporting cellar wall of a much later structure.

The two arches of the church of the Annunciation of St Mary in the Newarke, possibly part of the crypt, reappeared in 1936 when excavations were taking place in preparation for the foundations of a new wing for the Hawthorn Building of the Leicester College of Art. Previously, the remains could only be seen deep within the cellars of adjoining buildings facing Asylum Street. Although there had been many phases of development over the centuries, they appear to have defined a boundary of land ownership, which has probably contributed to their survival while the buildings around them have been lost.

The Hawthorn and High Aston Buildings

Some years before construction work began on the original phase of the Hawthorn, the Leicester artist Thomas Elgood recorded the scene that he knew was soon to vanish. In the background are the rooflines of Skeffington House and (far left) Wyggeston's Chantry House, both of which are now part of the Newarke Houses Museum.

The Chantry House was built in about 1511 by William Wyggeston to house two chantry priests who sang masses for his soul in the nearby church of St Mary of the Annunciation. The chapel was demolished soon after its closure in 1548, but the Chantry House survives as possibly the only Elizabethan urban gentry house in the country. The chantry priests serving St Mary de Castro had their own house nearby. It is now a music technology studio for

The Arches of St Mary's in the Newarke

The only surviving stonework from the church of St Mary of the Annunciation in the Newarke, revealed when the site was cleared before the construction of the final phase of the Hawthorn Building.

De Montfort University, having been used for many years as a storeroom by the shoe manufacturers Portland Shoes. This building as it exists today is probably sixteenth century in origin and was later used as the vicarage of St Mary de Castro. Before its near-total demolition in 1949 it was a three-storey, three-window stone house with a slate gable-ended roof. All that remains now is the ground floor.

Until recently, little was known about Hugh Aston's life and times except for references in A. Hamilton-Thompson's history of the Newarke church and college published in 1937. However, research by Professor Patrick Boylan, Professor Emeritus of Heritage Policy and Management at City University, London, is fostering renewed interest in this fascinating man and his music.

Aston studied music in Oxford and worked in the city for some years. He was at the Newarke College by 1525 as the 'Keeper of the Organs' and 'Master of the Choristers' and remained in Leicester for the rest of his life. It is possible that Aston had been 'poached' from his previous employment, as the Newarke College had acquired the privilege, apparently shared only with the Chapels Royal, of having the right to recruit outstanding musicians and singers from other institutions without their consent.

Aston lived just outside the precincts of the Newarke in a rent-free house, almost opposite the Newarke Gateway and also outside the south gate to the town. After the dissolution of the College, that property appears to have remained in Aston's ownership and was inherited by at least two generations of his descendants.

Within a few years of his arrival in Leicester, Aston had taken on a more secular role outside the college. He represented the Southgates Ward as a member of the town council and later as a Borough Alderman. He was a Justice of the Peace, the auditor of accounts and mayor of Leicester for 1541/42.

This remarkable man was clearly of great learning but must also have been a busy and personable character, successfully bridging any barriers between the religious and the secular, fulfilling his daily commitments to the services in the Newarke while undertaking roles of considerable responsibility in the 'outside world'. Finally he became one of the two Members of Parliament for the Borough of Leicester in the Parliament of 1555, and he remained an Alderman until his death.

Aston was buried on 17 November 1558 in the parish church of the Southgates ward, St Margaret's. Some of his music lives on and is available on commercial recordings. A small part of his repertoire

The Skyline of Leicester, 1937
An evocative view of Leicester's rooftops from high up on scaffolding during the construction of the fourth wing of the Hawthorn Building in the Newarke. Factory chimneys abound. The spire of Leicester Cathedral can be seen on the horizon, with the cottages next to Trinity Hospital in the foreground.

Wyggeston's Chantry House
William Wyggeston built this house around 1511 for two priests who sung Masses for his soul at the nearby church. The only Elizabethan urban gentry house in the country, it has changed considerably over the years. The third floor was added in the later sixteenth century. It was used mainly as a private dwelling until 1940 when it was damaged by bombing. It was later used as an office.

has been performed in the chapel of the Trinity Hospital, where Aston may once have conducted his own work, and more of his music could be heard by guests attending the formal opening of the University's Hugh Aston Building.

Originally known as The Municipal Technical & Art School, the Hawthorn Building was later named after Mr J. B. Hawthorn, who was appointed permanent headmaster of the school in August 1898. He retired in 1924. The name is historically coincidental in that Henry, Earl of Leicester, provided his church with a thorn as a holy relic.

The School of Art from which De Montfort University grew began its life in a small house in Pocklington's Walk in 1870. The Revd James Went, the first headmaster of Wyggeston Boys' School, began a series of day and evening classes teaching technical subjects when the school was opened in 1877. The classes were not listed as official school subjects. The subjects included engineering, building and machine drawing. They were probably financed on a voluntary basis, and pupils were entered for Department of Science & Art examinations.

In 1881, the Leicester Chamber of Commerce proposed that a Technical School should be established. A sub-committee was formed, and a group of members, including James Went, visited a number of technical schools in Yorkshire.

On 12 June 1882, the Chamber of Commerce's Technical Education Committee made a formal proposition that a Hosiery School be established to begin in the autumn of that year, offering evening classes in geometry, geometrical & mechanical drawing, physics & mechanics freehand drawing, technology of spinning, technology of framework knitting, and practical framework knitting. The classes were to be held in Wyggeston Boys' School, and no rent would be charged.

James Went persuaded the governors of the school to contribute £1,000 for an extension to the buildings. The new construction was to memorialise Mr Edward Shipley Ellis, whose house in the Newarke stood where the Hawthorn Building now stands, facing Trinity Hospital. The extension was opened on 20 November 1884, under the name of the Ellis Technical School. At that time classes in hosiery and the boot and shoe trades were begun, and by 1887 practical classes in pharmaceutical chemistry were running. For some years, Wyggeston's House, opposite the school, was brought into use to provide additional classrooms.

In November 1891, the committee controlling the school of art requested that the town council took over the running and funding of the school. Although initially the controlling committee of the Technical School preferred to continue as they were, a decision was

The Newarke by Thomas Elgood, 1896
The character of this area of the Newarke has changed greatly over the centuries. This romantic watercolour of gardens and elegantly dressed young ladies is by the Leicester artist Thomas Elgood. The street in the foreground is on the line of Grange Lane.

Magazine Square
This is the same view as in Elgood's painting, photographed in 2012. The rooflines and chimney stacks of Skeffington House have changed very little.

made on 30 August 1892 to purchase from the trustees of the deceased Edward Shipley Ellis his former residence and land in the Newarke for £7,500. A building should be erected to house both schools – student numbers then stood at five hundred in the School of Art and one thousand in the Technology School.

The result was the opening of the Hawthorn Building on 5 October 1897, and all classes in both disciplines were taught there. The Revd James Went retired in 1920 after serving education in Leicester for forty-three years. More students and a steadily increasing demand for courses required three further extensions to Hawthorn between 1909 and 1936.

Mosaics

Leicester City Council commissioned Sue Ridge, an artist based in the East Midlands, to design a series of colourful mosaics to cover the subways which linked the Newarke and the city beneath the Central Ring Road. The designs were then brought into physical being by ceramics expert Christopher Smith.

Sue had worked on public art across the country, but the majority of her work can now be seen in the city of Norwich. She also teaches and is well known for her work in hospitals. As can be seen, the mosaics were often intricate, decorative and pleasing to the eye. Many of the panels were brightly coloured but others were designed with more subtle hues. Sue has talked about her approach to her art: 'My work considers place and audience, private thoughts and public moments. My approach to site is through investigation and research: what makes a place specific, memorable?'

For the Newarke mosaics, Sue took her inspiration from the work and life of the sixteenth-century Danish astronomer Tycho Brahe. Born Tyge Ottesen Brahe in 1564, Brahe made a catalogue of over 1,000 stars. His work as an astronomer was remarkably accurate for his time. Most importantly, it had a significant impact that remains today.

In May 2011, NASA issued an X-ray image on the internet of 'Tycho's supernova remnant'. This same celestial body was referred to by Shakespeare in *Hamlet* as 'yond same star that's westward from the pole'. In 1572 when the light from this explosion first became visible on earth, it was a world-shaking event: a new star that had not appeared on any previous star charts, and one so brilliant that it was visible even in the full brightness of day.

In Denmark, Tycho Brahe made precise observations of the star which was later to be named after him. Brahe's observations were

Newarke Gateway and Mosaics
The Newarke or Magazine Gateway towers above the modern ground level in this photograph taken from the subways of the 1970s. The mosaic tiles of the former Newarke subways complement the chequered brickwork of the fourteenth-century building.

The Tycho Brahe Mosaic
This was the centrepiece of the Newarke mosaics, and was located near to the junction of Southgates and Vaughan Way (the Central Ring).

revolutionary and provided confirmation of an emerging scientific understanding of a dynamic universe. This was in contradiction of the prevailing Ptolemaic system, which stated that all celestial bodies were unchanging and fixed in place.

One of Sue Ridge's larger mosaics, which was situated on the eastern sloped footway near Millstone Lane, depicted Brahe's early view of the universe, the moon revolving around the earth, the planets revolving around the sun, and stars on the edge of the known universe.

When they were made, the Newarke mosaics were some of the largest in the country. The mosaic segments were extremely colourful, bringing a real sense of drama to something as mundane as a city centre subway, but towards the end the plague of graffiti had taken its toll.

The policy of using subways to connect areas on either side of busy roads was challenged by town planners in the 1990s. Subways, by their very design, were vulnerable to vandalism as well as the elements. Lighting systems often failed due to water seepage and these structures became very costly to maintain. They also became a focus for crime because of their isolation.

Consequently De Montfort University proposed a scheme to reroute the part of the Central Ring Road that, since its construction, had isolated the Newarke Gateway. Also included in the scheme was the filling-in of the subways, which were replaced by controlled pedestrian crossings. The price to be paid for putting right the clumsy town planning in Leicester in the 1960s was the loss of the mosaics, which now lie buried beneath many tons of rubble infill.

three

IN THE STEPS OF
JOSEPH CAREY MERRICK

Joseph Carey Merrick trod the streets of Leicester for some seventeen years before his voluntary incarceration in the Leicester workhouse. The area of Leicester in which he lived and worked has changed greatly over the years, but several very tangible structures that have a direct association with Merrick can still be found within that small area of habitation.

His time in the town, almost twenty-three years of his thirty years of life, was a period of incessant misery and pain. He experienced both psychological and physical cruelty because of the attitude of others to his disfigurement, but at times he was also befriended by individuals who showed him great kindness, respect and understanding.

He was born on 5 August 1862 at his family home at No. 50 Lee Street in Leicester. His parents lived in Lee Street for only three years before, like many in this poor district, moving on, in search of a lower rent or greater prosperity. Joseph Rockley Merrick had married Mary Jane Potterton just a few days before the end of 1861. Their first child, Joseph Carey, was born seven months later. Before his third birthday, the family had moved on, to Upper Brunswick Street, in the same neighbourhood.

Throughout his comparatively short lifetime Merrick conducted himself with great dignity. He enjoyed social intercourse, valued literature and was himself very literate. In his autobiography, he tells us that he went to school 'like other children until I was about eleven or twelve years of age'. This comment is significant; most children at that time left school at the age of thirteen, and it seems likely that his somewhat earlier departure from the education system coincided with the death of his mother.

Mary Jane Merrick died on 19 May 1873. Undoubtedly, Joseph had been very close to her. She too had some form of physical disability, which had given even greater strength to the bond between her and her son. He was devastated by her passing. She was not only his mother, but also the one person in whom he could confide and find love and comfort. Her death also brought about a change in the family's dynamics, as later in the following year his father remarried, and from that time he became a stranger to what remained of his family.

Lee Street

Lee Street ran from Wharf Street to Bedford Street in an area of closely packed residential streets lying between the main routes from Leicester to Belgrave and to Humberstone. Built on low lying land, the buildings often flooded, and the inadequate drainage and sewerage led to much ill health. Wharf Street was the principal route through the area, serving as the local 'high street'. Today, the Lee Circle multistorey car park lies across the original path of Lee Street, and only the western section of the street remains – a turning off Bedford Street, used now as the entrance to a surface car park. Where the tarmac has worn away in some areas of this car park and on the road itself cobbled surfaces can be seen, which presumably date from when the street was a busy residential area.

The buildings in Lee Street in the Victorian period were a mix of narrow back-to-backs and small shops, numbered from the Bedford Street end. Merrick's birthplace and first family home would have been at the opposite end, very near the junction with Wharf Street, on the north-west side of the crossroads with Gladstone Street and immediately opposite the theatre that was later to play a short but significant role in Merrick's life.

Parallel to Lee Street and separated from it only by the width of two back-to-back houses was Hill Street. In the 1930s, the Charles Street job centre was built between the two roads at the junction with Bedford Street, and it was near here, at No. 9 Hill Street, that Joseph secured employment, rolling cigars for Freemans, a tobacconist.

The entire length of what remains of Hill Street is now pedestrianised and flanked on the city-centre side by Epic House, an office block and retail development built in the 1960s on the site of the former Leicester (or Leicestershire) horse repository. This building, in the Victorian Gothic style, dated from 1932, when the present Charles Street was constructed. An earlier repository, close to the junction of Hill Street and Bedford Street, was demolished at this time.

The purpose of the repository may have changed over the years, but one can imagine in earlier times the stage and mail coaches arriving from the north, passengers disembarking and horses being fed and watered. With a constant flow of travellers from Lincoln,

Lee Street
The cobbled surface of the alleyways and yards off Lee Street near to Bedford Street are still evident in the twenty-first century.

Lee Circle
Lower Lee Street in 2013, seen from its junction with Bedford Street. The Lee Circle car park is in the background. The rear of the Charles Street job centre can be seen on the right.

Loughborough, Newark and Nottingham, various ancillary businesses such as Freemans the tobacconist grew up around the repository to serve them – very much in the same way that a modern motorway service area operates today. Merrick worked here for about two years, between 1875 and 1877, but then, in his own words, 'my right hand got too heavy for making cigars, so I had to leave them.'

The Workhouse

The workhouse was never far from the thoughts of the thousands of people who lived in the Wharf Street area. The Leicester workhouse was close by, on the opposite side of the Humberstone Road. It was built to house the increasing numbers of men, women and children who sought relief due to unemployment – no less than 19,000 individuals in 1847/48. It was gaunt, rambling and retained an imposing and daunting entrance lodge from the earlier workhouse, which stood on the same site.

Merrick met with William Cartwright, the administrator of the Leicester workhouse, in December 1879 after working for a short time as a door-to-door hawker. It was a tough and seemingly hopeless role for a man with such a disfigurement. People refused to open their doors to him, were frightened by his appearance, or hurled abuse at him. His meagre takings dwindled steadily until, after one confrontation with his father when he had been severely beaten for failing to bring home enough money, Merrick abandoned all hope of finding a form of employment that was open to him. He turned his back on his family and walked to the workhouse. He was admitted on 29 December 1879.

The iron gates through which Joseph Merrick walked on that day still stand. Today they can be seen in Sparkenhoe Street, on the boundary of Moat Community College. The narrow gates allowed for one person to enter or leave at a time, in the manner of a turnstile. Two gatehouses guarded the entrance to the lodge, one on either side. Those approaching would sense the prison-like atmosphere, and if they looked up they would see the forbidding façade of the workhouse lodge – a tall, three-storey building, its height emphasised by even taller chimney stacks and mock lookout towers. When Merrick entered, he joined over 900 individuals who were already there.

The workhouse later became Leicester's Hillcrest Hospital, though little effort was made to hide its history. The hospital closed in 1974 and the buildings were finally demolished in 1977, but even at that late stage many of the original workhouse fittings existed, including heavy stone boulders with iron hoops set into them where violent

The Leicester Workhouse
The gaunt and imposing frontage of the workhouse lodge, at the time when the building was in use as Hillcrest Hospital, around 1960.

inmates had been restrained. Some months later, Moat Community College was constructed on the same site. There were extensive cellars under the workhouse, and some of these remain today. Several of the external walls of the college match the lines of the walls of the former building precisely, possibly because the remaining cellars dictated to some extent where the foundations of the new building could be laid.

Remarkably, on 22 March 1880, Joseph left the workhouse of his own volition. His intentions are not fully known, but presumably he believed that he was able to secure some form of employment. However, just three days later and destitute he returned, this time to remain within those walls for four years.

Gladstone Vaults

On 29 August 1884, Joseph Merrick ate his final meal in the workhouse, and this time he knew he would not be returning. The Hippodrome theatre, also known by several other names, including the Gladstone Vaults, a familiar building from his childhood, was about to become a significant milestone in his career. Merrick had engineered a contact with Sam Torr, the owner of the theatre. He had written to him from the workhouse to suggest that his disfigurement might be to their mutual advantage, offering himself as some form of stage freak show.

The theatre had a long and chequered history although it would have looked comparatively fresh and modern to Merrick's eyes. It was built in 1862 as the Gladstone Hotel & Concert Hall, but it never prospered, and over the years it was to bring financial ruin to several would-be entrepreneurs. Less than four years after its construction, the first owner, William Cooper, sold it on to a Samuel Sweeney, who consequently became bankrupt. It was offered for sale again in 1867, 1869 and in 1872, when it was being used as a mission hall under the title of the Gladstone Hall Ragged School.

Arguably Sam Torr was its most colourful manager. He opened the building on Monday 3 September 1883 as the Gaiety Palace of Varieties, and Leicester's own Vesta Tilley topped the bill. Sam came from Nottingham, and before becoming a licensee of Leicester's Green Man public house he had made a name for himself on the London variety stage.

After visiting Merrick in the workhouse, Torr agreed to his request, and set up a group of four theatrical businessmen to develop Merrick's 'career' including appearances at the Gaiety Palace. It was this group that gave Merrick the title the 'Elephant Man', and it was this partnership that would take Merrick to London.

The Gates to the Workhouse
The original Victorian gates to the workhouse on Sparkenhoe Street have survived, next to a modern electricity substation.

The Workhouse Lodge and Gatehouses (c. 1880)
The two brick gatehouses add to the sense of imprisonment and the generally unwelcoming character of the workhouse. The men and women are probably members of staff, as they seem too well-dressed to be inmates.

However, it was Sam Torr who was to face unaccustomed hard times. Business at the Gladstone Vaults declined, and it began to lose money. Torr managed to sell the building two years later, and by 1895 it was under new management again, this time as the New Empire Theatre of Varieties.

It has been suggested that the wrong sort of 'clientele' was attracted to the limelight, because it is rumoured that the adjacent building at No. 27 Wharf Street, later to become famous as Lief's pawnshop, was at that time being used as a brothel, servicing some of those who used the theatre next door as a convenient alibi for their activities.

At this time, Sam Torr's daughter, Clara, kept a diary in which she recorded the last days of her family's involvement in the building that was their life and livelihood:

> Everything was going lovely as we thought. We had a manager. He looked like a parson and knew about as much as one concerning the profession. We had several barmaids sometimes taking farthings for half-sovereigns. We had several waiters always missing when they were wanted. We also had a chairman which they played all kinds of jokes on ... But the crash came all too soon. One morning my dear Mother came to me in terrible distress saying, 'Clara, everything will be sold in a few days and we shall be homeless. Whatever will become of us?'

By the time Clara and her family had to leave Wharf Street, Joseph Merrick was in London, and 'performing' as a sideshow freak with entrepreneur Tom Norman acting as his manager. Only a matter of weeks after leaving the workhouse in Leicester he was to meet Sir Frederick Treves, the surgeon who was to become his friend for the rest of his short life.

The New Empire Theatre of Varieties in Wharf Street struggled on for some forty more years, but the theatre lights finally dimmed soon after the First World War. In place of live theatre came the big screen. In 1922, the Hippodrome became a picture house, and later changed its name to The Empire. At last, the building had found its niche in the lives of the people of the area, and it prospered through until the 1940s. In the 1950s, the building fell into disrepair. It is not listed in Kelly's 1957 Street Directory. In the 1970s the upper storey was removed, and it was converted into a retail shop.

The old building survived long enough to have its brief association with Joseph Merrick recorded at a modest public ceremony, when

The Gladstone Vaults
The former location of the Gladstone Vaults in 2012, on the corner of Gladstone Street and Wharf Street, opposite Merrick's birthplace. The cellars, which were used as dressing rooms, can be seen below the street level.

a granite plaque was unveiled in his memory by the Lord Mayor of Leicester on 15 May 2004. It was paid for by the Friends of Joseph Carey Merrick, who campaign to publicise the work of those who support people with Proteus Syndrome. However, planning permission was granted for redevelopment of the building in March 2008, and it was subsequently demolished on Friday 20 March 2009.

The upper frieze, which was constructed of stones carved with theatrical motifs, was saved from destruction. It was discovered that each stone was numbered on the reverse. One stone was auctioned through the internet to raise money for the work of the Friends of Joseph Carey Merrick. The others are still in storage in a demolition yard in Leicester.

The plaque was removed and taken into storage until the 'Friends' secured a new permanent location for their commemoration of Merrick on the exterior wall of Moat Community College. It was presented to the students and staff at a short but moving morning assembly on 1 December 2011.

The Gladstone Vaults

Known also as the Hippodrome, the Gladstone Vaults on the corner of Wharf Street and Gladstone Street ended its days as a Motor Factor's retail shop. The original carved frieze, with theatrical motifs, can be seen at the roof level.

Wharf Street Shops and Lee Street (1934)

This view of shops in Wharf Street is very close to Merrick's birthplace. The fish and chip shop (left) is on the corner of Lee Street. Merrick was born two doors away at No. 50 Lee Street.

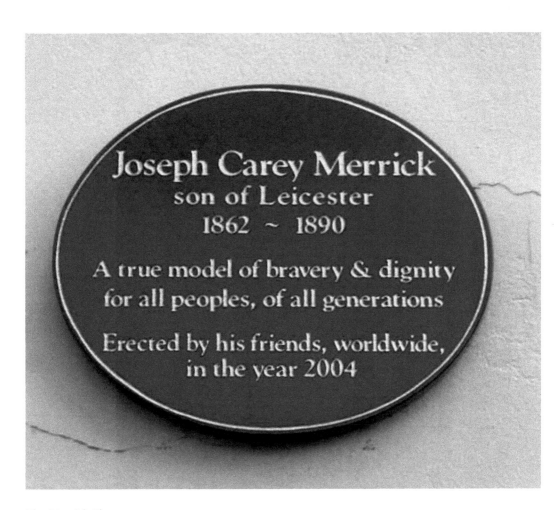

The Merrick Plaque
Donated by the Friends of Joseph Carey Merrick, the granite plaque was first placed on the wall of the Gladstone Vaults on Gladstone Street. It is now permanently displayed near the entrance foyer of Moat Community College, the site of the workhouse.

four

THE BEGINNING AND
THE END OF THE LINE

From the start, the railways dramatically changed the landscape of England. Even the earliest lines involved major engineering projects, including tunnels, embankments and bridges. Although in places the route of Leicester's first line has been obliterated, the physical evidence remains.

Leicester was in at the start of the railway age. It was one of the first towns in the country in which a railway line was constructed. George Stephenson's line between Stockton and Darlington opened in 1825, and its success encouraged other areas of the country to reconsider earlier opposition to railway development. Stephenson's Liverpool & Manchester Railway opened in 1830, but by then he and his son, Robert, were already in discussion with landowners, mine owners and engineers in Leicestershire, with a view to constructing a line that would link the coalfields of north-west Leicestershire with the town of Leicester.

Their first meeting with the businessmen of the town, led by William Stenson, a mining engineer from Coleorton who developed Whitwick Colliery and is regarded as the 'founder' of the town of Coalville, took place at the famous Bell Hotel in Humberstone Gate. The detailed and serious discussions that took place resulted in the opening of the Leicester & Swannington Railway just two years later on 17 July 1832, although the line did not reach Swannington until 1833.

A transport link from the mines in north-west Leicestershire was much needed, to enable coal to be brought into the town and thence taken onwards to the major residential and industrial areas. The Leicestershire pits were in fierce competition with those in neighbouring Nottinghamshire, which had the benefit of a canal network for transporting the extracted coal. Attempts to develop a similar network in Leicestershire had collapsed with the failure of the Charnwood Forest Canal. Carrying such a heavy commodity as coal by road was difficult, as for many months of the year the carts would find the heavy clay of Leicestershire unable to bear the weight. The eventual construction of the line was similar in method to that of the canals – a series of relatively level sections of track connected by short inclines, as in the locks of the canal system, where trucks were winched from one level to the next by rope.

The Leicester terminus of the line was beside the wharf at West Bridge, where coal could be transferred to the Soar Navigation. Today, the area is dominated by the road traffic system of St Nicholas Circle around the Holiday Inn, indicative of the dominance of the motor vehicle since the latter decades of the twentieth century. The canal is still evident, and some Victorian factories and mills have survived along the route of the waterway. The remnants of that first railway terminus can still be seen, close by the canal, near to Tudor Road and King Richard III Road, but it is now an inauspicious memorial to a great engineering achievement, neglected and marred by vandalism and graffiti. The surviving platform is original, from when the railway's owners decided to carry passengers, and the trackbed is now a public footpath running for about a mile towards the Glenfield tunnel.

The terminus was rebuilt several times, and initially it was not intended for passenger use. It was not until 1893 that any facilities, including a platform, were provided. The local investors in the line bought up a number of useful buildings, including some rural inns, along the route which were later brought into use as ticket offices and waiting rooms. The early travellers were required to purchase their fare at one of these buildings, and the 'ticket' was in the form of a metal token, handed in at the destination.

The Steam Whistle

A collision took place on Saturday 4 May 1833 on a level crossing east of Leicester, between Bagworth and Thornton, when the engine driver Martin Weatherburn drove the engine *Samson* into a cart containing 50 lbs of butter and eighty dozen eggs that was travelling to Leicester market.

Martin Weatherburn was the son of Robert Weatherburn, a longstanding engineering friend of Stephenson, who was the first man to drive a locomotive on the Leicester to Swannington line. Martin first worked on the railways in Liverpool and then followed his father to Leicestershire. His youngest son, Harry, was born in Leicester. Harry, after his father's death in 1868, travelled to Australia on board the SS *Great Britain* and worked on the railways there.

West Bridge Station
A view of the Leicester end of the line in the days of passenger trains. The first platform at West Bridge was built in 1839, seven years after the line opened. This photograph was taken around 1895, soon after the first passenger station had been built.

The End of the Line
The West Bridge station in 2012, a neglected memorial to a major engineering project.

An earlier collision involving the locomotive *Victory* colliding with *Comet*, another locomotive, led to Weatherburn being suspended for a time, because it was found that he had been driving too close behind the leading locomotive. This adds some weight to the suggestion that the later incident with the market cart might have been the result of reckless driving.

Although no one was injured, the accident was deemed serious enough to warrant Stephenson's personal intervention. One account states that he had 'mouthblown his horn' at the crossing in an attempt to prevent the accident, but that no attention had been paid to this audible warning, perhaps because it had not been heard.

Stephenson subsequently called a meeting of directors and accepted the suggestion of the company manager, Ashlin Bagster, that a horn or whistle that could be activated by steam should be constructed and fixed to the locomotives. Stephenson later visited a musical instrument maker in the Duke Street area of Leicester, who on Stephenson's instructions constructed a 'steam trumpet', which was tried out in the presence of the board of directors ten days later.

An extensive search of street directories of the period has failed to produce any evidence of a musical instrument maker in this area of Leicester, but it is possible that Stephenson actually commissioned a local organ builder to construct his whistles. The fact that this new device could have been constructed and demonstrated in just ten days suggests that it was not designed from scratch, but employed some instrument that was already available. Again, there is no record of an organ builder in the Duke Street area, but certainly there were a number of them in the town at that time.

Stephenson mounted the whistle on the top of the boiler's steam dome, which delivers dry steam to the cylinders. The device was apparently about 18 inches high and had an ever-widening trumpet shape with a 6-inch diameter at its top or mouth. The company went on to mount the device on its other locomotives.

Although some commentators credit the Cornishman Adrian Stephens (or Stevens in some accounts) as the inventor of the steam whistle, it is more commonly agreed that this event on Saturday 4 May 1833 led to the invention of the steam whistle mounted on and connected to a railway locomotive. The true story may be that Stephens should be credited with the invention of the device, but failed to patent it. Stephens died in 1876 in Merthyr Tydfil and no patent for the device existed in 1865.

There is another account that sets the invention of the steam whistle against the actual opening of the line in 1832, rather than associating

West Bridge, *c.* 1835
A very rural image of the earliest form of railway passenger services from Leicester, with no waiting room and no porters.

Campbell Street Station
The dramatic and inspiring Grecian-Revival-style entrance to the Campbell Street railway station, which opened in 1840. Compare the scale and grandeur of the architecture with the modest structures at West Bridge.

it with a specific incident. A cannon was fired that had been specially cast for the opening of the Leicester & Swannington Railway to salute the new steam locomotive *Comet* on its inaugural run (driven by Robert Weatherburn). It is said that a stationmaster who was present for the ceremony and celebration suggested to Stephenson that all new locomotives should have some kind of audible warning device. Stephenson agreed, and a local man who made musical instruments was commissioned to design and to build a prototype 'steam trumpet'.

Steam whistles were used in other industrial applications. Factories used whistles to announce the beginnings and ends of shifts, steam tractors used whistles to call for more coal or water, ships used whistles signal to other vessels, even small machine shops and foundries used small whistles as signals of various sorts.

Some specialised whistles were used as fire alarms and others were used on steam-powered fire engines. The Liverpool & Manchester Railway adopted steam whistles on their locomotives, not by following the example of the Leicester to Swannington line, but after a visit by a member of their staff to Dowlais Iron Works in 1835 where a device designed by Adrian Stephens was in use.

Steam whistles work by releasing steam into chambers called pitch pipes. Small chambers produce a higher musical note, and larger chambers produce a lower note. Most steam engine whistles used a combination of pitch pipes (usually six different sizes) to produce a musical chord.

Railway Architecture

The Glenfield tunnel is a remarkable feat of early railway engineering, and one that still exists in good repair. Just over a mile in length, today it is owned by Leicester City Council, and over the years it has required costly and regular maintenance in order to protect the buildings on the land above from subsidence. During construction, engineers discovered that almost one third of its length would be through porous rock. This meant a lining was necessary, which had not been budgeted for. As with many similar projects, the tunnel was also costly on the human scale: the contractor Daniel Jowett fell down a shaft and was killed.

When it was opened, it was only the second tunnel in the world on a passenger railway. It proved so much of an attraction for the inquisitive that gates had to be fitted at either end to keep the sightseers at bay. On the opening day, the chimney of the locomotive *Comet* was knocked down because of the limited clearance in the tunnel. From then on, special rolling stock was constructed, and engines were fitted

Campbell Street Car Park Gatepost
One of the two surviving gateposts from the former Campbell Street station; they now mark the entrance to the London Road station car park.

Thomas Cook by James Butler
This fine statue of the tourism pioneer was unveiled in 1991. Cook had his original idea of universal tourism while waiting for a stagecoach in Kibworth Harcourt, some 10 miles away.

with chimneys that could be lowered. The first passenger coaches had bars over the windows so that passengers could not lean out. Later, a 'bypass' line was constructed between Desford and Leicester, via Kirby Muxloe, which connected with the Leicester to London main line approximately 1 mile south of the London Road station.

Undoubtedly, the grandest piece of railway architecture in Leicester was the Campbell Street station, opened by the Midland Counties Railway in 1840. The station was designed by Leicester architect William Parsons in the Grecian Revival style, with a tall and impressive main building embellished with a central pediment set forward on fluted columns in front. This was flanked by two short single-storey wings. This grand structure also served as the headquarters of the Midland Counties Railway until 1844 and contained the company's offices and boardroom on its upper storey.

This splendid building was demolished after the completion of the London Road station in 1894. Most of the site of the old station is now occupied by a public car park for rail passengers and by some parts of the Royal Mail parcels depot in Campbell Street. Some of the platforms of the later station are located in approximately the same position as those of the earlier station. Just one piece of the original structure has survived, namely the Egyptian-style gate pillars that serve now as an entrance to the car park.

The passengers who travelled on Thomas Cook's first privately chartered railway excursion, from Leicester to Loughborough on 5 July 1841, passed through this gateway, and walked up the steps of this grand station. This first arrangement with the Midland Counties Railway Company led to further excursions and finally to the setting-up of his own business.

Cook's association with this location is commemorated by the statue, designed by James Butler and unveiled in 1991, which stands near the junction of Station Street and London Road. Incidentally, it was in Kibworth Harcourt, some 10 miles south along the same highway that Cook first had his idea of universal travel. And it was around a mile uphill that Cook built his own private residence. No. 244 London Road, which Cook named 'Thorncroft', is now the headquarters of the British Red Cross in Leicester.

The Wyvern, designed by Leicester architect Arthur Wakerley, served as the 'railway hotel' to complement the London Road station, but it was never a commercial success because it was a temperance establishment. Close by, in Granby Street, Cook built his own temperance hotel and hall in 1853. The hotel was the first building in Leicester to boast piped water – from the reservoir at Thornton, which

The Cook Hotel and Temperance Hall
A contemporary artist's impression of Thomas Cook's two important buildings on Leicester's Granby Street.

The Thomas Cook Hotel
The Temperance Hall was demolished many years ago but the hotel has survived, although the ground floor has been heavily rebuilt. Leicester City Council agreed to the demolition of the hotel in 2008.

had been commissioned in 1854. The building was Cook's home for a time, and also housed his printing presses.

The temperance hall was demolished many years ago. The adjacent and less impressive hotel has survived, but was converted into a retail shop with little regard for its original façade. The threat of demolition has hung over the hotel for some time, as planners have agreed to a planning application to replace it and the adjacent buildings with an office block. However, the recent recession has to date given this important building a temporary reprieve.

The London Extension

The line that was to leave its mark most emphatically on the landscape of Leicester was the 'London Extension' of the Great Central Railway. It was the last complete main line to be built in England and as such was one of the most finely engineered, with gentle gradients and curves. It is also one of the best documented, as a full photographic record of its construction was made. Ironically, it was also the shortest lived of the main lines. Express passenger services were withdrawn in 1960 and the Leicester station was closed in 1969, just seventy years after it had opened. At the time it was the largest single building to have been erected in the town.

Across the central area of Leicester, the running tracks of the Great Central were raised on viaducts, embankments and bridges. Many of these structures have been demolished, but the sheer scale of the engineering enterprise has left sections still standing. The bowstring bridge at the junction of Western Boulevard and Braunstone Gate was the last major structure of the line in Leicester to be demolished, despite a vigorous campaign to save it.

The line between Leicester and Loughborough is now operated as a heritage steam railway, and part of this section is the only location in the United Kingdom where steam-hauled trains can be seen passing at speed. The Leicester terminus on this line is a new station, Leicester North, which was completed in 1991.

Apart from a brief interregnum in the early 1970s, Leicester can perhaps claim to be the city with the longest history of steam-hauled railway travel, which has spanned over 180 years since 1832.

five

HIGHCROSS STREET

The written history of Highcross Street spans at least 900 years, and for much of that time it was the major street in the town, linking the important routes into Leicester from the north and the south.

Until about the middle of the fifteenth century this was Leicester's high street, or *alta strata*, where important public buildings were constructed and significant events took place in the time of municipal power. Today it is still possible to walk from the site of the former north gate of the town, near to the present junction with Sanvey Gate, along the line of the street to the south gate. Indeed, the names survive. However, its dominance as a street declined from the early decades of the nineteenth century, and today sections of the street are known by modern names – Applegate and St Nicholas Place.

The unwritten history of Highcross Street dates as far back as the Roman occupation of the town, as its route follows closely the eastern boundary of Leicester's Roman forum. Close to the southern end of the forum, the street crossed the important line of the *Fosse Way*, arguably the most important and historic crossroads in Leicester's long history.

At the heart of Highcross Street, in the centre of the ancient town and marking the street's intersection with the route between the east and west gates, was one of Leicester's ancient markets. Today, the location of the old market cross is still marked in the tarmac and is passed every week by thousands of shoppers heading for the Highcross Shopping Centre.

The Leicester artist John Flower (1793–1861) recorded several scenes in and near Highcross Street in his important book of lithographs, *Views of Ancient Buildings in the Town and County of Leicester*, published in 1826. His eye for detail ensures that his work is still consulted today. One of his best-known lithographs is of the former market cross, close to the intersection of the modern Highcross Street and High Street, the site of one of the town's ancient markets. The Wednesday market, selling dairy produce, poultry, fruit and vegetables, had been held here from the twelfth century, and the Friday market, which sold bread, dated from the fourteenth century.

John Flower portrays the High Cross in a view which looks north along Highcross Street with the cross itself in the foreground and the old grammar school in the distance. Next to the grammar school, separated from the school by Freeschool Lane, is the dominant presence of the old borough gaol. A shop occupies the next plot, and then a public house.

This market survived until the middle of the nineteenth century, when it was transferred to the present Market Place, then more commonly known as the Saturday market.

The original market cross had a long history. In the mayor's accounts for 1314 is a record of payment for the rebuilding of the cross. Will Steyn was paid sixpence for 'going into the neighbourhood of Banbury for John the Mason' and a further elevenpence was given to 'a certain mason staying and making the nodes and vanes of the cross after Master John's departure'.

The cross was replaced in 1577 by a larger structure forming a canopy or shelter, a circular structure with eight pillars supporting a pointed roof. It was decreed that anyone hanging washing between its pillars was liable to a fine of one shilling. By the late eighteenth century, it had fallen into disrepair, and it was consequently sold off, section by section. Just one pillar remained to identify this historic place where the four streets from the town's gates intersected. It survived here until 1836 when it was sold to James Rawson, who paid for it to be re-erected on his land in the Crescent in King Street. In 1977, it was moved to Cheapside, near the present Market Place, and in 2012, the city mayor, Sir Peter Soulsby, announced plans to return it to its original location as part of broader plans for the historic enhancement of the area. It is this pillar that can be seen in Flower's lithograph.

The old borough gaol was a building with its own colourful history, probably not appreciated by its many transient occupants, and it was one of two such institutions overlooking the old marketplace. One was owned by the Borough of Leicester and one by the County.

The borough gaol was probably the oldest and was probably in existence by the late thirteenth century. A new facility was built in about 1614 on the junction of Highcross Street and Causeway Lane, near to the present Vaughan Way, which was rebuilt in 1792 at about the same time that the earlier gaol was demolished.

The High Cross by John Flower

We still remain indebted to the Leicester artist John Flower (1793–1861) for his careful and detailed lithographs and paintings of the town. He specifically selected views which he believed were soon to change or be lost.

The Borough Gaol

The demolition of the old borough gaol in 1880. The view looks south along Highcross Street towards the High Cross. A man can be seen climbing on the partly demolished wall of the old gaol. Was he a workman or a passer-by? We can only guess what he may have been looking for.

The county gaol had a similarly chequered history, having been rebuilt on several occasions. Finally, the stories of the two institutions merged when a new gaol for the borough was built on the site of the former county gaol in Highcross Street, close to the market cross. This was finally demolished in 1879 after being a heavy cost to the town for many years. It can be seen in Flower's lithograph. One narrow section of the gaol has survived between more modern frontages.

Land between St Martin's church, now Leicester Cathedral, and Highcross Street, was chosen by the Wyggeston family as the site of their hospital, but the story begins a little further to the north, beyond the old marketplace where the Free Grammar School still stands. This was established by Thomas Wyggeston, brother of William, and Agnes his widow, after William's death in 1536. Stone from the defunct church of St Peter's, which had previously accommodated the small school, was used in its construction. The new building was much needed, as records indicate that by 1572 most of the roof and timbers of St Peter's had been removed, except for the area of the south aisle where the school was housed. Queen Elizabeth I gave a donation to the new school, and this gift no doubt prompted Leicester's wealthiest citizens to follow suit.

After being used by a number of businesses, including the former Barton's bus company, this building of great character has been carefully restored, and is now a restaurant, and a part of the Highcross Shopping Centre. Further stone from St Peter's, rediscovered in archaeological investigations before the shopping centre was constructed, was used during its refurbishment.

The later Wyggeston Boys' School was built on land between Guildhall Lane and Peacock Lane in the nineteenth century, but the association between the Wyggeston family and that land is 500 years old. It dates to 1513 when the plot was chosen and subsequently acquired by the Wyggestons as the site of a hospital.

The Wyggestons (or Wigstons) were wealthy and prominent wool merchants in Leicester for hundreds of years and they no doubt originated from the town of Wigston just a few miles south of Leicester. They rose to prosperity during the fifteenth century, but they had been merchants in the area for several centuries before then. The hospital and school that they founded are still important and active elements of the city of Leicester today.

It is William Wyggeston, brother to Thomas and Roger, who is the most prominent member of the family. He traded in wool, from whence came his fortune. Throughout his life he inherited and maintained considerable commercial interests in Leicester, Coventry and the port of Calais, where he was mayor on four occasions. His activities in the prosperous wool trade made him the wealthiest man in Leicester of the time. The subsidy roll for 1524 shows that he owned over 20 per cent of the taxable property in the town. His assessment for taxation was no less than six times higher than that of the next richest resident, who happened to be his cousin, also named William and also a former mayor.

Wyggeston obtained the necessary authorisation to establish his hospital by letters patent in 1513 and 1514. Originally, the foundation was intended to provide accommodation for twelve poor men and two chaplains, but twelve poor women were added to that number at a later date. The land adjoining Highcross Street and next to St Martins' church was purchased in 1513, and by 1518 the hospital and its ancillary buildings had been constructed. The hospital was called the Hospital of William Wigston Junior, and it was dedicated to the Blessed Virgin Mary, St Katherine, and St Ursula and her companions. The two chaplains who were to be appointed had to be chosen by either William or his brother.

William Wyggeston made sure that his hospital was financially secure by endowing substantial tracts of land, which he purchased between 1513 and 1520. This land included manors in Castle Carlton in Lincolnshire and Swannington in Leicestershire, together with other land in Leicestershire, Lincolnshire and Staffordshire. His widow, Agnes, later bequeathed the lease of tithes in the town's South Field, and a further sum of money, to the value of £100, was included in William's will.

The qualifications for admittance to the hospital were very clearly set out in the phraseology of the time. They were to be either 'blind, lame, decrepit, paralytic, or maimed in their limbs, and idiots wanting their natural senses, so that they be peaceable not disturbing the hospital'. It was also prescribed that they had to be unmarried and without the support of any friends or relations. The twelve women were described as 'poor, aged, and of good report and honest conversation'. The male patients were selected or admitted by William or his brother and the female patients by either William or Agnes.

The chaplains were to say Mass daily at times convenient for the poor, either in the morning or evening. On Sundays and on all the principal feast days, matins, vespers, and other offices were to be recited in the presence of the poor.

There was an immediate association with St Martin's church. The hospital was responsible for the maintenance of two chantries, in essence to pay for two priests to celebrate Mass for the soul of the departed. One of these was for Thomas Smyth, a draper in Leicester, and was to last seventeen years from Christmas 1525, paid for from funds left by Smyth for the purpose. The second was for William Breyfield and was to last fourteen years from 1533.

In the hospital, the men lived in individual rooms on the ground floor. The women were accommodated on the floor above, where there was also the provision for them of a common room. The patients were not permitted to leave the hospital grounds without permission and they were provided with weekly allowance and some clothing. The patients were cared for by three of the stronger women. Two of these women looked after the men, and the third cared for the remaining women. The duties included making the beds, undertaking the cooking of meals and attending to the personal cleanliness of the patients. For this they received a weekly allowance of 8*d* and the assurance of a place in the hospital if the day came when they themselves became in need of care.

The buildings constructed by William Wyggeston for his hospital in 1518 survived for over 350 years. They stood in St Martin's West, close to the west end of St Martin's church, the length of the hospital proper running parallel to the path of that name between Guildhall Lane and Peacock Lane.

It was a long building of two storeys, timber framed and covered with plaster with stone buttresses. The Master's House was located to the north, its exterior wall being where the wall now divides the car park of St Martin's Centre and the Guildhall. This was enlarged in 1730 by the addition of one storey and a sloping slate roof. A small stone Gothic chapel was located at the opposite end of the hospital, near to Peacock Lane. This was also restored in 1730.

The hospital building also contained rooms for the nurses. A second set of buildings was constructed later on the western side of the hospital, containing storerooms and kitchens. The Confrater's House formed an extension at right angles to the main hospital building, with an entrance on Highcross Street, and completing a form of quadrangle was a courtyard and gardens.

The chapel contained a significant quantity of painted glass, most of which was removed to the parish church of Ockbrook in Derbyshire at the beginning of the nineteenth century. Some of the windows were blocked up at the same time. The chapel also contained the tombs and monuments of several of the masters and confraters, including that of the first master, William Fisher.

The last inmates left the buildings in April 1868 and the old hospital then lay empty for almost eight years. In that time, a powerful debate over the future of the buildings raged. Then, in May 1874, the character Highcross Street between Guildhall Lane and Highcross Street changed dramatically.

The ancient Nag's Head public house had stood at the junction of Highcross Street and Guildhall Lane since at least 1662 and had retained its original wooden porch. Further along Highcross Street was the Confrater's House constructed in the sixteenth century. Next were a number of small – and possibly rather dilapidated – residential properties dating to the middle of the eighteenth century, and then at the corner of Highcross Street and Peacock Lane stood the old Peacock Inn. It was announced that all were to be demolished in the month of May in 1874.

Worse news was to come for those who were campaigning to save the original Wyggeston buildings. After more than a year of apparent inactivity but in July 1875 the announcement was made that 'the whole of the valuable building materials in the Wyggeston Hospital Buildings, St Martin's West, including a splendid old and massive timbered oak roof, oak moulded Gothic doors' were to be sold by auction.

On Monday 9 August 1875 the auction took place. The proceedings were reported in the local newspapers and the buildings were demolished 'without delay', according to the conditions of sale. Handcarts were used by the purchasers to remove stone and other items from the site. The materials and fittings were sold for £92. The tombs and memorial slabs from the chapel were removed to the new chapel. The seats from the chapel were given to the Trinity Hospital, and the porches that had faced the path in St Martin's West were given to St Nicholas's church, together with a niche from the chapel. Two wood porches in St Martin's West, which had carved upon them the rebus of William Wyggeston, were not included in the sale. These porches were given to a member of the Leicestershire Archaeological & Historical Society to be donated to the church of St Nicholas nearby.

The Leicestershire Archaeological & Historical Society had campaigned vigorously to prevent the demolition of the hospital, proposing that it could be used as the assembly hall for the intended new school. The eminent local historian James Thompson addressed the society on the issue at their Annual General Meeting:

> The proposal to demolish the Hospital of William Wyggeston in this town, with the chapel at its southern extremity, and, consequently, to disturb the remains of the dead lying beneath the floor of the chapel, involves consequences so serious that it behoves the Leicestershire Architectural & Archaeological Society, which professes to regard

the preservation of ancient architectural remains as one of its chief objects, to consider well whether it can in any way ward off the blow, or whether it must stand by and witness in silence, and without remonstrance, the threatened violation of the tombs of the dead, and the uncalled-for destruction of one of the few remaining monuments of the piety and charity of the departed benefactors of this ancient borough.

The site of the old chapel can still be seen today. Some of the stone footings above the modern ground level exist in the corner of the car park of St Martin's Centre between St Martin's West and Peacock Lane. In earlier years, when the buildings were occupied by schools, this area was protected by iron railings.

The Old Grammar School
Also known locally as the Elizabethan Grammar School. It may seem inappropriate that this building has been used as a warehouse or as an office for a bus company, but this fact has probably guaranteed its survival into the twenty-first century.

The Site of Wyggeston's Hospital
The site of Wyggeston's Hospital became the playground for Wyggeston Boys' School and is now the car park of St Martin's Centre. This view is similar to the archive image on page 5.

The Wyggeston Statue, the Clock Tower
We have no pictorial record of William Wyggeston, so his statue on Leicester's clock tower, completed in 1868 by the local architect Joseph Goddard, is purely a Victorian 'impression' of this great man of Leicester.

six

NO. 9 ST NICHOLAS PLACE

Although the address is modern, this is the story of a plot of land in the oldest part of Leicester. The story of this land begins with the arrival of the invading Roman forces in AD 48. Initially, this was a military occupation, and it was sometime later that a civilian town with public buildings would develop. Eventually, a forum was constructed, flanked by streets on at least three sides. To the east of the forum, a main street ran from the north gate to the south gate of the walled town. The north gate was located where Highcross Street today intersects with Great Central Street, before the junction with Sanvey Gate. Today, that north–south route runs beneath part of No. 9 St Nicholas Place.

Our understanding and knowledge of the layout and extent of the Roman town is being extended all the time by archaeological research, and it is clear that St Nicholas Place, formerly a section of Highcross Street, respects the eastern boundary of the Roman forum. However, at some time in the past Highcross Street veered to the west, to reach a new south gate, approximately where today's Southgate intersects with the Central Ring, near to the Newarke Gateway.

No doubt such a prime location in the Roman town, so close to the most important public buildings, would have been a much sought-after address for upwardly mobile Romans, and evidence of Roman occupation of the site can be seen today, off Guildhall Lane, opposite the Guildhall and beneath No. 9 St Nicholas Place.

How the town fared in the centuries following the end of the Roman occupation is a matter of debate and a subject for further research. Clearly, the larger Roman structures would have survived for some time after the – gradual – departure of the Romans, unless they were consequently deliberately demolished. Whether for some time the town was uninhabited is a matter of conjecture, but continuity can be seen in the surviving grid structure of the streets, which is embedded in the road map of Leicester in the twenty-first century.

Yet, that part of St Nicholas Place (as it is referred to today) which serves as an extension of Leicester's modern High Street towards St Nicholas Circle, does not respect the Roman forum. St Nicholas Street, as it was known until the 1960s, crosses the location of the northern end of the forum.

It is easy to speculate, and current knowledge can only be based on what has been discovered through archaeological excavations; but it would seem that a remnant of the population stayed in the town and, without any overall or coherent strategy, made use of some of the structures left behind by the Romans. The gateway entrances to the Roman town were important and dictated the natural places where people would continue to go into and out of the town, and so Highcross Street, connecting the north and south entrances, survived as a conduit for merchants, travellers and, perhaps, Saxon speculators.

Another key route, established early in the Roman occupation of the area, was the Fosse Way, which connected the military outposts guarding the then northern limits of their occupation. Leicester was one of those outposts. The line of the Fosse Way, approaching Leicester from the south along what is known today as the Narborough Road and exiting towards the north along Belgrave Gate towards Thurmaston, passes through the town close to the southern boundary of the forum, and skirts the very edge of No. 9 St Nicholas Place, possibly linking the west gate (the route and bridge over the River Soar from the west) and the east gate (near to the clock tower and following the line of Haymarket and Belgrave Gate).

Today, that junction is near to where Guildhall Lane adjoins Highcross Street and is the corner where No. 9 St Nicholas Place is located. An 1828 map of the area shows the site laid out as cultivated land, traversed by a number of paths. There is an indication of a turning off Guildhall Lane (then Town Hall Lane) approximately opposite the guildhall, running behind the site.

Some indication that the area was still at the heart of the town as late as the seventeenth century is gained from an account in the borough records dated 3 February 1820, when the death of King George III was proclaimed at a number of important places in the town. The High Sherrif made the proclamation first at the castle and then proceeded up Highcross Street to be joined at the end of Town Hall Lane (the southern end of the BBC site) by the mayor and corporation 'in their full formalities preceded by the Town Waits and surrounded by the Constables'. The party then marched past the front line of the site to the High Cross. A similar procession

No. 9 St Nicholas Place
The BBC studios were completed in 2005. Their modern design merges successfully with the remnants of the former Victorian buildings on the corner of St Nicholas Place and Guildhall Lane.

Wathe's, Highcross Street
The same location as the above photograph, but with a different address. The former Wathe's store was used for some years as an Antiques Centre before its partial demolition in 2004.

followed exactly the same route on 30 June 1830 to mark the death of King George IV and his succession by William IV.

Underneath the building and extending beneath the pavement along Guildhall Lane is an undercroft which relates several chapters in the history of the site. This remarkable structure was hidden from view and from knowledge for many centuries until the Victorian period, and was then largely forgotten until an unfortunate accident in the 1980s involving a later occupant of the building.

It was revealed for the first time in many centuries by workman in 1861 who were constructing a warehouse for Robert 'Paddy' Swain and Joseph Roberts of Nos 21/23 Highcross Street, who were wholesaler grocers in Leicester trading under a variety of names and in partnership with other merchants including Thomas Almond and John Latchmore. Swain, Almond & Latchmore went through several company changes including Swain, Almond & Goodliffe and R. P. Swain & Co. Paddy Swain was a well-known local character.

Dr John Barclay, who was the President of the Leicester Literary & Philosophical Society in 1857, gave a lecture to the society in 1864 in which he refers to the construction of the building. He noted the panels of encaustic tiles mounted on the front elevation facing Highcross Street, a unique use of such decoration in Leicester at that time.

After the Second World War, the building was used for several different businesses. Thomas Herbert Wathe took over the larger section facing Highcross Street, and his business also had a retail store facing onto the adjacent High Street. Wathe's claimed to be the first dealership in the area to sell Chevrolet cars! They are listed as T. H. Wathe & Co. Ltd, electrical engineer, in the street directories of that time, their address being Nos 3–7 Highcross Street. Wathe's worked with the major refrigeration manufacturers of the period, including Frigidaire and Neff. The management of Wathe's expected total loyalty from their workers and to some extent were seen as dictatorial.

Next door, on the corner at No. 1 Highcross Street, was the company Block & Anderson Ltd, described as a retailer of business systems and best-known for its 'Banda' duplicating system. In the side of the building on Guildhall Lane, facing the Guildhall, were L. Bell and Co. Ltd, printers, and W. Mann & Co., wholesale grocers.

The rise of the national electrical retail chains signalled the end of Wathe's as a shop. Despite offering a more personalised customer service, they found it impossible to compete with the discounted prices of the new chains, and finally they were forced to close their doors.

Guildhall Lane by John Flower
This view of Guildhall Lane, looking towards Highcross Street, was used for reference by archaeologists working on the site where the new BBC studios were to be constructed, immediately opposite the Guildhall.

The Undercroft, 1861
The remarkable structures beneath No. 9 St Nicholas Place were uncovered in 1861 during construction work on Swain & Latchmore's cigar warehouse.

Ironically, one of their major competitors was Currys, another company that had begun in Leicester. Wathe's continued, however, providing refrigerated display units to the new generation of supermarket stores. In their heyday, the warehouse manager of Wathe's had difficulty finding space for his stock, which included bulky items such as refrigerators and television sets, so he stored goods below ground, in the cellars that, a century before, had kept Paddy Swain's cheese and port wine cold and fresh. He made full use of all the space available to him, including the medieval undercroft and the tunnels that ran beneath Guildhall Lane.

By the 1970s, the buildings were being used as a repository for second-hand furniture, trading as the Antiques Complex. The corner shop became a restaurant under several owners and names including Café Canton, Hello Canton and the Noodle Bar. The Noodle Bar closed in 2009, and the premises were taken over by the Clockwise Credit Union.

It was a relative of the two brothers that ran the Antiques Complex who 'rediscovered' the undercroft. The area above was used at the time as a yard for delivering and collecting furniture. Understandably, some of the vehicles that parked there were of considerable weight. It was while a van was being loaded that the ground gave way and a woman fell through to the level below, fracturing her leg. The accident was reported in the *Leicester Mercury*. It prompted renewed interest in the undercroft, and in 1989, for the first time in many years, an archaeologist squeezed himself through a limited opening and explored the remains waiting below. In the following year the Leicester Archaeological Unit, led by Richard Buckley and Jules Hagar, undertook a detailed survey.

In 2001, land agents purchased the entire site on behalf of the BBC and work began on the construction of a new broadcast centre for BBC Radio Leicester. The old Victorian buildings, by this time in a very poor state, were demolished. However, the panels of encaustic tiles from the frontage were retained and relocated inside the new building. Additionally, that part of the original building running along the corner of St Nicholas Place and along Guildhall Lane was renovated and designed into the new centre.

Before construction work began, a team from the University of Leicester Archaeological Services (ULAS), led by Roger Kipling, undertook a major survey of the site, resulting in a comprehensive published report as well as a catalogue of fascinating photographs of the excavations and finds. It is a story that begins in the first quarter of the twelfth century, when the undercroft was constructed

The Cigar Warehouse
An artist's impression of Swain & Latchmore's building appeared on the front of the boxes of cigars sold and distributed by the company. The perspective chosen presents it as an imposing structure, but in later years it became almost unnoticed in the midst of the redevelopment of the area.

No. 9 St Nicholas Place, 1972
The importance of Highcross Street as the centre of trade waned over a long period of time as the commercial heart of the town moved eastwards towards Gallowtree Gate. This photograph from 1972 shows the former cigar warehouse, neglected and ripe for demolition.

on top of 'dark earth' deposits. Rebuilding and extensions took place between the fourteenth and sixteenth centuries, and a timber-framed building was built on top of it sometime between 1550 and 1775. The undercroft itself measures internally about 8½ metres by 4½ metres, and its floor is about 2½ metres below the modern street level. It is mostly of granite but with some green sandstone and reused Roman brick and tile. There are the remains of four windows in the wall to the west and intriguing square niches in the west and north walls lined with Roman tile, which may have housed candles or lamps.

It seems possible that this structure would at one time have been owned by a wealthy merchant, who may have resided in an adjacent building fronting Highcross Street. The location is significant because this individual would have lived and worked next to a major road junction, the intersection of the north–south 'high street', and the east–west Fosse Way. This would have been a prime location from which to operate a business, but one that could have been secured only by a man of considerable wealth. The undercroft is built in part over a third Roman street running north–south, parallel to Highcross Street, suggesting that by this time the street had become redundant or forgotten, perhaps obliterated by debris. If this was not the case, then it would have constituted a significant appropriation of a public space for private use, an act that could have been accomplished only by someone of high status, wealth and influence.

The topping-out ceremony for the new broadcast studios took place in March 2004, and the first full day of live BBC Radio Leicester broadcasts took place on Saturday 9 April 2005.

In 2006, members of the Tiles & Ceramics Society (TACS), led by Denis Gahagan, were invited to view the encaustic tiles, which were now on display within the BBC Centre. The tiles were already known to the Society; its intervention prior to the demolition of the old building had ensured their survival. They confirmed that one of the designs was by Maw & Co., but that its usual context was as part of a church floor. Another panel, the largest, was identified as being by Minton & Co., and a third, showing the royal coat of arms, is very similar to one at Malvern Abbey and was manufactured by Walter Chamberlain, whose firm was superseded by Maw & Co. TACS agreed that these configurations were a very early example, if not the first, of the fashionable early usage of encaustic tiles on a façade. Inside the BBC building, these Victorian tiles have been complemented by several specially commissioned items of public art, designed by ceramist artist Cleo Mussi.

The Antiques Centre, No. 9 St Nicholas Place
An unusual view of the same building dating from the 1960s, looking through the arched entrance from Highcross Street into the central yard.

The Undercroft, No. 9 St Nicholas Place
The undercroft is revealed once again, this time in 2004 during a detailed archaeological survey.

The reason for their inclusion in the original building design remains a mystery. It could have been some gesture to the historic location, as the frontage of the building looked out across to where the Roman forum once stood and where many Roman mosaics could no doubt once have been seen; or perhaps it was simply the case of a Victorian builder offloading a job lot of tiles from a previous project.

The undercroft has also survived and is now protected. As building work commenced, this ancient space was capped with a layer of concrete after lights and CCTV cameras had been installed. The remains are accessible, but health and safety issues prevent regular visits. From a room off the central atrium of the centre, a reinforced glass panel set in the floor allows a glimpse of the archaeology beneath, and observant viewers may also see a piece of paper on which one of the archaeologists has typed a message for the future, asking that this little corner of Leicester's history be protected and cared for.

The Undercroft, No. 9 St Nicholas Place
Another view of the excavations on the site of the former Wathe's building undertaken in 2004 by ULAS.

The Highcross Street Tiles
The tiles from the Highcross Street frontage of the Victorian building, now *in situ* within the BBC studio building. The precise location of this display is immediately above the Norman undercroft.

Cleo Mussi Mosaic
A detail from the fascinating mosaic that dominates the atrium of the BBC studios at No. 9 St Nicholas Place. The centre is open to the public on weekdays during office hours.

seven

LOST PLACES AND FORGOTTEN PEOPLE

There are many names that have, over many centuries, played a significant role in the development and character of the city of Leicester and that linger in the corporate memory of Leicester people. There are the entrepreneurs such as Nathaniel Corah, shopkeepers and traders including Wilkinson, Curry and Adderly, and religious reformers including William Carey and Frederic Donaldson. Four celebrated names are commemorated by Leicester's clock tower, namely Simon de Montfort, William Wyggeston, Thomas White and Gabriel Newton, and some are immortalised by the buildings that stand today as the legacy of their work, such as Vaughan College.

In some instances, memorials to these pioneers are hard to find or easy to overlook. Sometimes they may be in the form of a street name, but often it is something less obvious, such as the shell of a factory building or a stone sculpture hidden behind a wall. Sometimes it is simply a memory of the atmosphere and the life of a certain space in the city, where the buildings themselves no longer exist: buildings such as the Wyvern Hotel, next to the railway station in London Road; Filbert Street, the original home of professional football in Leicester for over a century; or the stadium in Blackbird Road where greyhounds ran on the same circuit that on the previous night had witnessed the roar of speedway bikes.

Some of their names may not be as familiar as those that have in former times have had their names lit up in neon in the High Street, but their influence remains and their work is recognised far wider than the boundaries of the city.

This chapter is a reminder of some of these former citizens of the town who, through their skills, faith and practical endeavours, changed the character of Leicester, sometimes significantly and sometimes in a smaller but still valuable way.

William Carey

Across the world, churches, colleges and schools bear the name of William Carey. Yet in Leicester, where he lived and preached, the only surviving memorial to the great Baptist missionary, founder of the Baptist Missionary Society and translator of the Bible into many languages, is a worn and disfigured sandstone bust that is to be found on the inside of the boundary wall of Wyggeston's House in Applegate, opposite the St Martin's Centre. It was totally obscured by vegetation until 2012, but since then the city mayor, Sir Peter Soulsby, has initiated a clean-up of the garden, and the sculpture can be seen once again, although behind locked gates.

William Carey was born in Paulerspury in the neighbouring county of Northamptonshire in 1761, the son of a shoemaker. He became a Baptist in 1783. From 1785 to 1789 he was the pastor at nearby Moulton, before moving to Leicester in 1789 to take up the calling of minister of the Harvey Lane chapel. He stayed for four years, living in the cottage opposite the chapel and supplementing his income by shoemaking and running a small school.

Carey was largely self-taught, but became fluent in Greek, Latin and Hebrew as well as knowledgeable in science and history. While in Leicester he wrote his impressive treatise *The Enquirer*, which has been described as the finest missionary treatise ever written. The Baptist Missionary Society was founded in 1792, largely as a result of Carey's influence. The following year, he travelled with his family to India. He worked as a foreman in an indigo factory in Calcutta and later established a church there before moving to Serampore in 1799. He was made Professor of Sanskrit and Bengali at Fort William Cottage in Calcutta in 1801 and in 1805 opened a mission chapel there. He was a prodigious translator, responsible, with others, for translating the Bible into six Indian languages and the New Testament into twenty-three more. He died at Serampore in 1834.

Harvey Lane, where Carey lived and worked in Leicester, ran from Redcross Street to Thornton Lane in the heart of the old town. All three roads were obliterated in the Central Ring development of the 1960s and now lie beneath St Nicholas Circle. The path of Harvey Lane lies close to the western frontage of the St Nicholas Circle multistorey car park, facing the reception area of the adjacent Holiday Inn. A blue plaque marks the approximate site of Carey's cottage, opposite the hotel reception. Just before it was demolished, a short informal and poignant ceremony took place at which a descendant of Carey, the Revd Hubert Janisch, blessed the building.

Blackbird Road Stadium
An atmospheric view of the former Blackbird Road greyhound and speedway stadium. This view is from the timekeepers' box and shows the speedway teams and cheerleader at the commencement of a race meeting in July 1974.

William Carey Relief Portrait
The weathered and much eroded limestone relief of William Carey, now located in the perimeter wall of Roger Wigston's House.

Harvey Walk, the pedestrian bridge and footway over St Nicholas Circle, is close to the site of the chapel and cottage. The chapel was situated at the north-east corner of Harvey Lane and Thornton Lane, opposite the cottage. It was built in 1760 and closed in 1845, but it reopened in 1864 after having been used as a school and a mission. In 1921, it was badly damaged by a fire but reopened yet again in 1924 as the Victoria Road Mission. In its latter years it was the home of Winterton's Slipper Components Ltd, a leather manufacturer, and had by then been renamed Carey Buildings. It was finally demolished in 1963. The stone bust of Carey, which had been inset into the front wall of the chapel above the entrance, was all that was rescued. It was relocated to the inside of the modern retaining wall of Wyggeston's House. The various relics that had constituted a small museum in Carey's cottage are now at the Central Baptist church in Charles Street.

The Vicar of the Unemployed

The Revd Frederic Lewis Donaldson was a preacher of a different generation, who looked no further than to the factory next to his church in Belgrave Gate for the focus of his ministry. He became the vicar of St Mark's in 1896. His parish was a landscape of poverty in the shadow of Leicester's dynamic textile industry. Donaldson wrote of his parish: 'There is represented much of the tragedy and pathos, shame and horror of modern social conditions – infant mortality, child labour, underpayment or sweating of men and women, decadence of physical life, consumption and premature death.'

He was, by instinct and later by his theology, a Christian Socialist, and he was later to play a leading role in the Leicester March of the Unemployed to London of 1905, at which time he gained the unofficial title of 'vicar of the unemployed'.

Most dramatically, his liberation theology gained visual expression in a set of remarkable painted images that were installed behind the altar at St Mark's. The Scottish artist James Eadie-Reid (1859–1928) was commissioned to create the seven sanctuary images depicting Christ as the Apotheosis of Labour.

Eadie-Reid was born in Dundee in 1856. He studied at Edinburgh and exhibited at the Royal Scottish Academy and the London Salon. He designed stained-glass windows and murals for many churches in the north-east and the midlands. At the time of the St Mark's murals, Eadie-Reid was living in County Durham and working in Gateshead, an area that knew well the poverty of the working classes. It would seem that Donaldson's unusual commission was

William Carey Inscription
The inscription beneath the bust reads 'in this house lived William Carey, Missionary, 1789–1793', referring to Carey's cottage in the now demolished Harvey Lane.

Southgates Underpass Construction
The scale of the construction work for the Central Ring and Southgates Underpass in the early 1960s is evident here. Medieval streets including Redcross Street, Harvey Lane, Applegate, St Nicholas Street and Thornton Lane were completely destroyed and the underpass cut through the heart of the Roman town. Carey's cottage was located approximately where the white caravan stands, middle right in this photograph.

one that Eadie-Reid appreciated and understood. There is a further painting by Eadie-Reid in the church of St Peter in Highfields.

Eadie-Reid's remarkable murals at St Mark's are now hidden from view. After lying empty for several years, St Mark's was restored and converted to a restaurant in the 1990s.

No Encore for Corah

Although their extensive factory was close to St Mark's, Leicester's most famous textile name was associated closely with St Margaret.

The Corah family had lived in Leicestershire since before 1600, and, like many villagers, by 1800 the family had combined framework knitting with their farming enterprises in Bagworth in the north-west of the county. Nathaniel Corah was born in 1777. He trained as a framesmith and while still in his twenties established a small textile business in the nearby village of Barlestone.

The deterioration in the country's economy forced Nathaniel into debt. Although he sought to negotiate and promised to pay back all the monies he owed, one of his creditors demanded full payment. As a consequence, Nathaniel faced legal action and was imprisoned. On his release, anxious to pay his way, he became a worker in a gun factory in Birmingham.

Two years later, finding he was once again unemployed, Corah saw the potential for a new business. While he had been in prison, his wife and children had lived in Leicester. He saw there the growth in small stockingers and at the same time the dramatic growth in the working-class population of Birmingham. He saw that there was business potential in connecting this developing supply industry with an equally growing consumer base. All that he needed was a horse and cart and a level of quality control to ensure that what he took from Leicester to Birmingham to sell was consistently made well.

He began buying items of clothing from the Leicester manufacturers and conveying them for sale to the markets in Birmingham. By personally selecting each item, he was able to establish a high level of quality control that was quickly recognised by his customers. On Saturday mornings he would purchase goods offered to him at the Globe Inn in Leicester's Silver Street, which he would then transport to a small warehouse in Birmingham's Edgbaston Street.

The project was a success, and by 1824 Corah was able to acquire a block of buildings in Leicester's Union Street, which he extended in 1827. This factory unit pioneered the concept of organised production management in the city.

St Mark's Church Altar Murals
The remarkable Christian Socialist murals of Eadie-Reid in the chancel of St Mark's church,
Belgrave Gate. They are now covered over but protected.

St Mark's Church, Belgrave Gate
Standing proud in Belgrave Gate, near to the present Belgrave flyover, St Mark's was
completed in 1872 by Ewan Christian.

In 1830, Corah's sons, John, William and Thomas, joined the business, which then began trading as Nathaniel Corah & Sons. This far-sighted move ensured the firm's future development, because just two years later Nathaniel Corah died at the age of fifty-one. In his later and more prosperous years, Corah had been able to pay all the debts that had led to his imprisonment as a young man. However, he refused to make good just one debt – to the man who in 1815 had refused to listen to his pleas and had demanded his arrest.

The next twenty years saw continued success for the company, its expansion requiring a move to a purpose-built factory in Granby Street and then to the famous St Margaret's works on a 4-acre site near St Margaret's church. The foundation stone for this factory was laid by Edwin Corah, Thomas's son, on 13 July 1865, heralding the start of Corah's greatest years. A year later, Edwin's sister, Jennie Corah started the massive beam engine that provided the factory's power – the first textile factory in Leicester to be designed for integral steam-driven power.

By 1866, over 1,000 people were working at St Margaret's, and the buildings had been extended twice. The architect of the first part of the St Margaret's complex was William Jackson, of Lowesby Lane, Leicester. Originally, a factory yard stretched north as far as the canal, but by 1941 there had been no fewer than nineteen extensions to the original building, taking up all available land.

At the time of the move from Granby Street, the company had adopted an image of St Margaret as their emblem. She was a most appropriate symbol due to her association with wool, being a shepherdess martyred around AD 300. The emblem was patented by the company on the very first day of the 1875 Trade Marks Registration Act, and is therefore the oldest trademark for knitted goods in the world. For many years, her statue, which some have said is weeping, stood proud on a plinth high on the external wall of the factory, facing the present Vaughan Way. After the demise of the company and the sale of the buildings in the 1990s, she was removed, first to a location in the central courtyard and finally in 2008 to the churchyard of St Margaret's parish church, facing St Margaret's Way where the Corah memorial is located.

The economic hardships of the years following the First World War took their toll on the Corah operation. After years of consistent expansion, the company faced their first experience of decline. The Corah family was obviously well aware of the political context. In 1931, John Corah gave his public support for the national government, commenting that since its setting-up he had seen a noticeable

Corah's St Margaret's Works
An area of the large St Margaret's works of Nathaniel Corah & Sons, photographed in the company's heyday. The well-kept lawns are indicative of the wealth of the company.

The Corah Statue of St Margaret
St Margaret represented the Corah brand for many decades. After the company closed down, the statue was moved into the central courtyard for safekeeping. She is now in the churchyard of nearby St Margaret's parish church where the Corah family tomb is located.

improvement in the local trading situation and promising to expand his company's operation if this government's future was confirmed. However, by 1936 various branch operations in Birmingham, Newcastle, Cardiff, Leeds, Manchester, Liverpool, Glasgow and London had closed, production being centred on Leicestershire. Profit margins were reduced and overheads cut. The firm was managing to survive, but their saviour came in the form of another saint, St Michael, of Marks & Spencer fame.

There are various stories regarding the origins of the company's highly profitable association with Marks & Spencer, but one point is frequently emphasised: such was the high standing of the Corah name that it was the high street retailer that approached Corah, rather than Corah seeking the help of Marks & Spencer.

In 1926, the retailer had chosen a new strategy. Previously, the company had pegged their prices, mindful of their origins in the 'penny bazaar' of Leeds Market. However, this had recently led to a reduction in the quality of the merchandise, in order to maintain the low prices. Finally, Marks & Spencer decided to take the potentially dangerous step of increasing prices in order to offer better quality goods. They were looking for manufacturers with a 'name' for quality, and they found Corah.

The final decline of the textile industry in Leicester probably began with the dramatic changes in British society that took place in the 1960s. After the drabness and austerity of the post-war years, the decade saw an explosion of new ideas and philosophies and a greater sense of freedom. Freedom of expression, as exemplified by the new popular music of the Beatles, led to a desire for less conformity in dress. This was welcomed by some areas of the textile business, but others were caught unawares. While many British manufacturers and retailers were still offering good-quality but conventional attire, the modernising companies of the developing world and the Asian subcontinent were starting to provide clothing that was of inferior quality but decidedly brighter, cheaper and trendier.

This was of course was only one factor relating to the industry's decline. There were many other pressures bearing down upon the old names in the business. There was the need to keep modernising in order to remain competitive, and this meant a constant need for finance in order to invest in new technology and machinery. Meanwhile British workers, faced with continuing inflation, demanded better rates of pay. Corah and their competitors were faced with the need to raise finance in order to survive while having to keep prices low and pay their workers more. Further pressures came from the powerful

The Corah Statue
After some years of neglect, the Corah statue of St Margaret now has a new resting place.
It is most appropriate that she now stands beside St Margaret's Way and in the churchyard
of her parish church.

Nathaniel Corah's Memorial Stone
Most of the St Margaret's complex still survives, though badly damaged by vandalism
and fire. Some areas are now home to new small businesses. Some physical references to
Nathaniel Corah's heritage can still be seen.

retailers, who demanded highly efficient manufacturing operations and very high standards of production. Just one failure to meet these standards could result in cancelled orders and financial ruin.

One former young employee of Corah at St Margaret's, who worked with the team that maintained the steam engines so vital to the continuous production of the factory complex, later used his skills to weld steel tubes and construct bicycles. He opened a shop near Leicester's clock tower at the junction with Haymarket. It was this man who went on to found the Currys chain of high street stores.

Former employees of Corah in more recent times will recognise the meaning of the phrase 'no encore for Corah'. *Encore* was the title of the company's staff magazine.

Filbert Echoes

In November 1940, the German Luftwaffe turned their attention to Leicester. Possibly one of the intended targets was the St Margaret's factory of Nathaniel Corah, which was in full production, working round the clock to produce socks and other clothing for British soldiers. The toll of the damaged and destroyed buildings included the main stand at Leicester City's Filbert Street ground, which had originally been constructed in 1921. By 1949 it was rebuilt, with much of the labour being supplied by German prisoners of war at a nearby camp.

The club, originally named Leicester Fosse, moved to Filbert Street in 1891. Since its formation in 1884, it had been based at five other locations in the town. Local legend suggests that the ground was first identified by a Miss Westland, the niece of one of the club's founders, Joseph Johnson (owner the famous department store that later became Fenwick in Market Street), after the Corporation had not renewed Fosse's lease on their previous ground at nearby Mill Lane, only weeks before their debut season in the Midland League.

The ground saw its record attendance of 47,298 for the fifth round FA Cup tie against Tottenham Hotspur on 18 February 1928. Spurs won 3-0. The last game to be played at Filbert Street was the final game of the of the 2001/02 season, which was also against Tottenham Hotspur. This time, Leicester gained a 2-1 victory. Matt Piper, who was born in Leicester, scored the winning goal – the last competitive goal to be scored at the ground, bringing to an end 111 years of football at Filbert Street. Piper retired in 2008 and now trains Under-15s in Leicester. In 2011 he returned to football, signing for Oadby Town. The demolition of Filbert Street was completed in the summer of 2003.

Filbert Street, the Tunnel
The tunnel at Filbert Street, a view seen by many footballers but few fans. The notice beyond the entrance reads, 'grass grows by the inch but is damaged by the foot. Please keep off the pitch'.

Filbert Street, Main Stand
Construction taking place on the 'new' Main Stand at Filbert Street in 1921.

Alfred Adderly

Alfred Adderly opened his draper's shop in the Market Place in 1856. His grand store in Gallowtree Gate was an extension of his first premises, as it was built on adjacent land.

Although Adderly's in Gallowtree Gate ceased to trade as a business under its own name in the 1920s, it is still regarded by many Leicester people as the epitome of old-style traditional department stores. It was, in the words of Professor Jack Simmons, 'the most highly esteemed of all the Leicester drapers, an embryo department store'.

For those who sought a career in Leicester's stores, Joseph Johnson's and Morgan Square had reputation and appeal, but all aspired to join the staff of Adderly's. This image is of Stockdale Harrison & Son's original architectural design for the store in Gallowtree Gate and dates to the first decade of the twentieth century. By that time, many of Stockdale Harrison's designs were being created by Stockdale's son Shirley, who, with Harold H. Thompson, designed De Montfort Hall in 1913.

In the 1920s the store was taken over by Marshall & Snelgrove but continued to trade under the Adderly's name until after the war. By 1947, the store was being listed in trade directories as Marshall & Snelgrove (Adderly's). The store closed after a serious fire in 1970. It was by then a part of the Debenhams group.

Joseph Herbert Morcom

On 29 November 1530, Cardinal Thomas Wolsey, charged with treason and on his way to London to face certain execution, fell ill and died in Leicester. He was buried in Leicester Abbey without a monument to mark his grave. Some 300 years later, his tragic association with Abbey Park was commemorated in the form of a statue by Joseph Morcom.

Morcom had been born near Wrexham in 1871 and arrived in Leicester in 1910 when he was appointed modelling master at the Leicester School of Art. He later purchased Pearson & Shipley, a firm of stonemasons and monumental sculptors based in the Newarke, which he renamed the Plasmatic Company. For the rest of his career he worked for the company, as well as sculpting independently and teaching at the Leicester School of Art.

His small stonemason's yard was situated behind the Trinity Hospital in the Newarke, near to where he was teaching and opposite the ornamental ironwork business of the Elgood family. In addition to his statue of Wolsey, he also created an image that would become an icon for many football fans walking to matches at Filbert Street – the popular Liberty Statue.

Gallowtree Gate, 2012
The former site of Adderly's store in Gallowtree Gate is seen here from a different angle. The replacement for Stockdale's impressive frontage can hardly be seen as an improvement.

Alfred Adderly, Gallowtree Gate
The original architect's drawing of the store in Gallowtree Gate, by Shirley Stockdale of Stockdale Harrison.

The idea to place a version of the famous Statue of Liberty on top of a shoe factory in Leicester was a result of a visit to the USA by the directors. Lennard Brothers Ltd was established in 1877 by five brothers: John, William, Fredric, Samuel and Thomas. Their first factory was on the corner of Deacon Street at No. 85 Asylum Street, now known as Gateway Street, in the Newarke. During the First World War, the company worked at full production providing footwear for the military. When the conflict ended, the management was faced with the challenge of reorganising the business to respond to the new domestic demand for shoes. Accordingly, in February 1919 two of the company's directors, Disney Barlow and Samuel Briers, travelled to New York to see how American footwear manufacturers were responding to the same challenge.

On their return, and inspired by what they had seen, the directors proposed that a statue of liberty be created and placed upon the roof of their new factory on Eastern Boulevard. Before the war, Lennard Brothers had patented the Liberty brand for a form of footwear they were beginning to market. With the approval of the Lennard brothers, they commissioned Morcom to create their iconic structure. It was carved from three blocks of stone at Morcom's workshop.

In the last two decades of the twentieth century, the factory on the corner of Eastern Boulevard and Upperton Road became empty and was damaged by vandalism. Eventually, the building was scheduled for demolition and the statue was removed and placed in storage. However, it was later renovated as part of Leicester City Council's regeneration scheme for the Upperton Road area, and on 17 December 2008 it was resited on the nearby Swan Gyratory roundabout. Attending the unveiling ceremony was Patrick Leonard, a descendant of the original brothers.

It now serves as a very noticeable landmark for visitors to Leicester, especially visiting fans attending football matches at the King Power stadium.

It is conjecture, but it would seem likely that the Lennards knew Joseph Morcom from their time in the Newarke before the war. The site of their former factory there is now part of the campus of De Montfort University, which grew out of the Leicester School of Art for whom Morcom worked. Although both the statue of Cardinal Wolsey and the Liberty Statue were created from several blocks of stone, they would have been very heavy to have been moved by road. Possibly they were transported to their locations along the River Soar, which passes through Abbey Park and in the other direction close to the Lennards' Eastern Boulevard factory.

Lennard Brothers' Liberty Poster
An early poster by Lennard Brothers
for its 'Liberty' brand of footwear.

The Liberty Statue
Liberty in her original location high
above the Lennards' shoe factory,
overlooking Eastern Boulevard and
the pathway to Filbert Street.

The Liberty Statue
Joseph Morcom's version of the famous Statue of Liberty, in its new location in the centre of the Swan Gyratory.

eight

THE CHANGING FACE OF LEICESTER

The landscape of our towns and cities changes constantly and often imperceptibly. It has probably always been the case. In about 1530, the antiquary John Leland wrote: 'the hole Toune of Leircester at this tyme is built of tymbre.' He was wrong, of course – we can list stone buildings that are still standing and that he would have seen. But that is how the town seemed to him at the time. Other visitors to Leicester have been equally dismissive of its architecture. J. B. Priestley found little to enthuse about when he visited in 1934, and Nikolaus Pesvner, in his *Buildings of England*, reported 'nothing of note in the High Street except perhaps Lloyds Bank,' and added 'there is nothing of interest in Gallowtree Gate'.

Buildings have a powerful effect on the landscape of towns. The right building in the right place can create a feeling of balance, continue a line of symmetry or add character and interest to an otherwise nondescript view. The inappropriate building can overpower and destroy the unity of existing structures. More importantly, buildings are for people. They each have a purpose relating to human existence and experience – for example, religion, education, manufacturing or habitation – and most are designed with this in mind. But, sadly, not always does the design take into consideration the effect of the building on those who will inhabit it or simply pass by it day-to-day.

Most buildings have a finite life. Events and attitudes may decide that a building's original purpose is no longer relevant or needed in a new age. Industries prosper and then fail; styles and standards change. Some of the buildings most resilient to change are the Victorian and Edwardian factories and warehouses, built at a time when energy and labour were both inexpensive commodities and available in abundance. Many are now finding new roles as inner-city apartments or residential care facilities, bringing people back into the heart of the city.

The concrete structures of the 1960s are probably the least resilient structures of our built environment, being constructed when there was less technical understanding of how concrete can be made and used, although this is a science that was well understood by the Romans. Even so, despite the abilities of the Roman engineers and the scale on which they built, it is to be noted that following the end of the Roman occupation, those still living in the area appear to have perceived their buildings as unusable or undesirable. Broadly speaking, the rectilinear street plan survived to influence later building, but the buildings themselves were largely left to decay, or were pilfered for their bricks and tiles. One could imagine a waste land similar to the newsreel footage of bomb-damaged towns and cities during the Second World War, but it is difficult to be certain of how those people of Leicester in the fifth to the ninth centuries lived, and impossible to know how much of the past they knew about and how they felt about it.

Although the rate of change in previous centuries may have been more gradual, there have been times and events in Leicester's history where the town has changed dramatically and quickly. There is some irony in the present concern for the protection of Leicester's Victorian buildings, given that the developers of that period presided over the destruction of more buildings than have been damaged or demolished at any other time in the town's long history.

Arguably, the most dramatic scheme to change the landscape of Leicester, which might have astonished even the Victorians, was the so-called 'Smigielski Plan' published in the early 1960s. Konrad Smigielski was the city's planning officer with a distinguished record of similar work in Europe. His plan for Leicester drew upon similar proposals in other English towns and cities and was certainly influenced by prevailing attitudes to both the future and the past.

Smigielski and his team had a quite specific view of Leicester's past, as a place where there was *little* change. He wrote:

In a sense, Leicester is a static city. Perhaps its motto *Semper Eadem* comes very near to the truth. Certainly it is not a city of radical change. For the most part its pattern of land use is well-established, having emerged gradually rather than dramatically.

However, Smigielski was also willing to note the view of Kenneth Browne, then the Features Editor of the *Architectural Review*. Speaking of the 'outsider', Browne wrote:

Only later does he realise the deep and lasting virtues that are the other side of *Semper Eadem*: an unhysterical balance, a willingness to accept new ideas, and a fair hearing for all points of view. These qualities have produced remarkable things.

The New Walk Centre
An example of the stark architectural concepts of the 1960s. The two tower blocks dwarf the surrounding older buildings. Originally intended for apartments, the building has been the home of Leicester City Council since the early 1970s. The centre is scheduled for demolition due to structural problems.

Smigielski's major concern was the management of vehicular traffic. He projected that in order to cope with the amount of traffic likely to pass through the city centre of Leicester in the future, new roads of motorway proportions would be necessary. His response, which was an idea he inherited from administration, and dates to the 1920s, was to route all non-essential traffic around the central area by constructing a new 'Central Ring'. A route for this new road had been mapped out some years earlier, but was amended.

Many of Smigielski's concepts are more easily accepted today than in his time. He initiated the pedestrianisation of Gallowtree Gate and Cheapside. His idea of connecting vital elements of the city by walkways is one that has received new support and validity from the city mayor, Sir Peter Soulsby. Smigielski proposed the connecting of the railway station with the clock tower area, and Cheapside and the market with town hall square.

The considerable opposition to these plans was from those who feared that the city they knew, with its red-brick façades, familiar lanes and friendly shopfronts would be destroyed. To some extent, they were correct. The plans included tower blocks of skyscraper proportions – dwarfing the genteel Victorian clock tower – and bold concrete bridges across the old streets. The fifteenth-century Newarke Gateway was to become an island between lanes of traffic on the new ring road, with subways, lit by plastic egg-box-like roof structures connecting the Newarke with the city.

The Leicester of the twenty-first century has inherited some of Konrad Smigielski's ideas. The concept of pedestrianisation has spread from the clock tower along Humberstone Gate, and along High Street. Where Smigielski failed – in limiting the dominance of the motor car – the planners of today are fighting back. The old Newarke Gateway is no longer an island in the middle of a ring road; the road has been rerouted to allow the building's historic association with the Newarke to return. And the dark subways that funnelled human beings beneath the dominant road traffic have been filled in. Today, the principle is that people take precedence over the car. Outside the railway station in London Road, a wide crossing now acts as a gateway to the city for visitors to Leicester. Beneath their feet is another defunct subway.

Another interesting and welcome outcome of late twentieth-century town planning in Leicester has been the resolution of the debate regarding the building materials of the future. Just as Leicester was transformed by cultural and technical influences into a town of brick and tile, then largely of timber, and then again of red brick, the 1960s saw the rise in the use of prestressed concrete. In the city its use is

The *Leicester Mercury* Building
Originally constructed in the early 1960s and intended to house England's first local radio station as well as the local newspaper, this building in St George Street was refaced in 2007/08.

Gallowtree Gate, 1960
Gallowtree Gate, looking towards the clock tower, with Adderly's store on the left and Boots on the right, when traffic and Leicester City Buses were permitted to drive along this route.

possibly most successfully represented by the Lee Circle car park, with its two intertwined but not linked circuits, similar to the now familiar double-helix model of DNA.

John Dean, a successor to Smigielski as Leicester's town planner, declared, looking out of his office on the top floor of the New Walk Centre, that 'Leicester is a red-brick city and always will be'. Ironically, the grey concrete twin towers of the New Walk Centre are scheduled for demolition because they are now structurally unsafe. Dean's view of a city of red brick is coming to pass, as many of today's buildings are faced in brick, made locally in the former mining areas of Leicestershire, around a concrete core.

Smigielski's plan was never adopted in its bold entirety, but its influence on future planning in Leicester was profound. The effect most detrimental to the city's heritage was the decision to tunnel the Central Ring beneath a new St Nicholas Circle. Smigielski's original idea was 'to create a strong and dramatic three-dimensional composition on this very important and strategically located site, forming a gateway into the city centre from the direction of the M1 motorway'. Its construction, extending over almost 5 acres, laid waste to a considerable area of the old town, wiped out centuries of archaeology and destroying entire streets and hundreds of buildings, dating from Tudor times through to the Victorian era.

The result has been of benefit to no one. The road system is not able to handle the amount of traffic trying to use it. The significant buildings in the area, such as the ancient church of St Nicholas, Vaughan College, the Jewry Wall Museum, Roger Wigston's House, and the castle park area are isolated, and the few 'new' buildings rising from the devastation consist of a hotel, a multistorey car park and a small service station. The hotel looks dated, the car park is dark and uninviting, and motorists found it so difficult to drive in and out of the service station that it closed some years ago.

It is because of the constant process of change that Leicester has its secrets. It is hoped that we are now in a new age of enlightenment with regard to the value that is placed on our heritage. The excesses of previous generations probably could not occur today, given modern planning procedures, but there is still the risk of buildings being lost due to neglect or because developers lack the finance required to make good use of them.

The future lies in the skill of the architects who can design buildings that will surprise and impress, but above all will create a place where human beings can live and interact.

Leicester in the 1920s

After the First World War, Leicester's major industries including textiles, boot- and shoemaking, and machine-building successfully adjusted to the post-war domestic economy. Red-brick Leicester is seen beneath the smoke of hundreds of factory and mill chimneys.

Lee Circle Car Park, 1970

One of the first multistorey car parks to be completed in Leicester, housing the first Tesco supermarket outside London on the ground floor. Its revolutionary design was featured in an English Pathé newsreel of the time.

REFERENCES AND
FURTHER READING

Many local history studies and volumes have been consulted in the writing of this book, including the familiar and important standard histories of Leicester. This is not an exhaustive list, but will provide the reader with some recommendations for further research and study.

Billson, Charles James, *Medieval Leicester* (Leicester: Edgar Backus, 1940).

Brown, Cynthia, *Wharf Street Revisited: A History of the Wharf Street Area of Leicester* (Leicester: Leicester City Council Living History Unit, 1995).

Burgess, Clive and Martin Heale (eds.), *The Late Medieval English College and its Context* (York: York Medieval Press, 2008).

Celebrating 100 Years – The Hawthorn Building 1897–1997 (Leicester: De Montfort University, 1997).

Elliott, Malcolm, *Victorian Leicester* (Stroud: Amberley Publishing, 2010).

Gahagan, Denis, 'Conservation News: The Panels at BBC Leicester', *Glazed Expressions, the Magazine of the Tiles & Architectural Ceramics Society*, 56, (Summer 2006), 12–14.

Hamilton-Thompson, A., *The History of the Hospital and the New College of the Annunciation of St Mary in the Newarke, Leicester* (Leicester: Edgar Backus for the Leicestershire Archaeological Society, 1937).

Harrison, Clive, *In Sickness and In Health* (Leicester: Leicester City Council Living History Unit, 1999).

Howell, Martin and Peter Ford, *The True History of the Elephant Man* (London: Penguin, 1980).

Kipling, Roger, 'A Medieval Undercroft, Tenements and Associated Buildings at 9 St Nicholas Place and Related Sites, Leicester', *Transactions of the Leicestershire Archaeological Society*, 84, (2010), 117–151.

Leacroft, Helen and Richard Leacroft, *The Theatre in Leicestershire* (Leicester: Leicestershire Libraries and Information Service, 1988).

McKinley, R. A. (ed.), 'The City of Leicester', *The Victoria County History of Leicester*, Vol. 4. (London, 1958).

Simmons, Jack, *Leicester Past and Present, Vol. 2: Modern City 1860–1974* (Methuen, 1974).

Simmons, Jack, *The Victorian Railway* (London: Thames and Hudson, 1991).

Sitton, Jeanette and Mae Siu-Wai Stroshane, *Measured by the Soul: The Life of Joseph Carey Merrick* (London: The Friends of Joseph Carey Merrick, 2012).

Skillington, S. H., *A History of Leicester* (Leicester: Edgar Backus, 1923).

Treves, Sir Frederick, *The Elephant Man and Other Reminiscences* (London: Cassel and Company, 1923).